How to Do Everything
Adobe® Photoshop® CS4

Chad Perkins

McGraw Hill

New York   Chicago   San Francisco   Lisbon
London   Madrid   Mexico City   Milan   New Delhi
San Juan   Seoul   Singapore   Sydney   Toronto

The McGraw·Hill Companies

Library of Congress Cataloging-in-Publication Data

Perkins, Chad.
How to do everything Adobe Photoshop CS4 / Chad Perkins.
p. cm.
Includes index.
ISBN 978-0-07-160522-9 (alk. paper)
1. Computer graphics. 2. Adobe Photoshop. I. Title.
T385.P4645 2009
006.6'86—dc22

2009005939

McGraw-Hill books are available at special quantity discounts to use as premiums and sales promotions, or for use in corporate training programs. To contact a special sales representative, please visit the Contact Us page at www.mhprofessional.com.

How to Do Everything: Adobe® Photoshop® CS4

1234567890 DOC DOC 019

ISBN 978-0-07-160522-9
MHID 0-07-160522-3

Sponsoring Editor	Roger Stewart
Editorial Supervisor	Janet Walden
Project Manager	Harleen Chopra, International Typesetting and Composition
Acquisitions Coordinators	Carly Stapleton and Joya Anthony
Technical Editor	Wayne Palmer
Copy Editor	Jan Jue
Proofreader	Madhu Prasher
Indexer	Karin Arrigoni
Production Supervisor	Jean Bodeaux
Composition	International Typesetting and Composition
Illustration	International Typesetting and Composition
Art Director, Cover	Jeff Weeks
Cover Designer	Jeff Weeks

As always, to Heefee and the kids.

About the Author

Chad Perkins is an award-winning software trainer, an Adobe Certified Instructor in Photoshop, After Effects, Encore, Premiere Pro, Illustrator, InDesign, and Acrobat, and is CompTIA CTT+ certified. Chad has authored multiple books on Photoshop and After Effects. He has trained or created art for such companies as Warner Brothers, Paramount, Nike, Sony, Lockheed Martin, Disney, and the United Way. Chad and his brother, Todd, broadcast the *All Things Adobe* podcast, which offers free tips in Adobe software: www.chadandtoddcast.com.

About the Technical Editor

Wayne Palmer owns Palmer Multimedia Imaging. He is a Photoshop and Photoshop Elements beta tester and has worked with Photoshop since version 3.0. He has been a technical editor for numerous Photoshop books and co-authored *Photoshop Restoration & Retouching, 3rd Edition*. Wayne also teaches digital imaging and Photoshop classes at the Pennsylvania College of Technology.

Contents at a Glance

Contents

Acknowledgments

The team at McGraw-Hill Professional has been fantastic to work with. Thank you to Roger Stewart and Carly Stapleton, as well as to all of the editors who caught my mistakes. It was a really great experience to work with Wayne Palmer as my tech editor again. His expert eyes always saw concepts that I missed. Thanks to Matt Wagner for being such a great support and advocate. Thanks also to my Seminary kids, who dealt patiently with the fact that I was a zombie every morning for two months. An extra special thanks also to my family, who frequently must endure my tendency to overbook my schedule. And yet, through all of this, they see the light at the end of the tunnel more easily than I do.

Introduction

Welcome to this book! Before we jump right in and start learning, I want to give you a heads up as to what you can expect going forward. If you're brand-new to Photoshop, or intimidated by Photoshop, have no fear. We'll go from the ground up. Even if you aren't quite sure what Photoshop does, or who uses it, or what jobs you can get with it, we'll catch you up to speed before you learn how to use it. Photoshop is not just for editing photographs anymore.

We'll then look at the *interface,* which is the layout of the buttons, features, and workspace of Photoshop. At that point, you'll feel comfortable enough to move on to the rest of the book, to actually start creating art.

If you have some prior experience with Photoshop, or if you are looking to use Photoshop for a specific purpose, feel free to jump around the book as you please. I've tried to create this book so that you can learn about whatever interests you, without having to drudge through material that doesn't.

This book also takes a different focus than most Photoshop books do. Other Photoshop books tend to focus on photo editing, which is obviously a core part of what Photoshop does (hence the name). And we will cover a lot of information about image editing, of course. But we'll also focus a lot on the creative side of Photoshop. For those of you who like to scrapbook, paint, design, or just be artistic, we'll cover many tools for the job. We'll even look briefly at using Photoshop for web graphics, 3D, mobile phones, and video.

Throughout this book, you'll notice that my screenshots are of a Mac computer. Note that Photoshop is available for both Mac and PC, and it functions almost identically on both. The real difference that you'll notice in this book is in the keyboard shortcuts. As we'll discuss, you can use combinations of keys to accomplish certain tasks in Photoshop much more quickly than you could otherwise. The keys usually used for this purpose are called *modifier keys.* These keys are different on Macs and PCs. For example, you can press the keyboard combination CONTROL (CTRL) and the letter o to open a file on a PC. On a Mac, you would use the keys COMMAND (CMD) and the letter o to perform the same function. Each time I refer to a keyboard shortcut, I'll give you both the PC and Mac shortcut. On the PC, the modifier keys are CTRL, ALT, and SHIFT. On the Mac, the modifier keys are CMD, OPTION, and SHIFT. Other than that, there really isn't much difference between platforms, except where noted.

1

Welcome to Photoshop

How to...

- Utilize the power of Adobe Photoshop CS4
- See the bigger picture of digital arts and Photoshop
- Use other creative programs with Photoshop

Hello, welcome to Adobe Photoshop CS4. You'll learn a great deal about Photoshop over the next few hundred pages. The world of Photoshop is exciting, and you might decide to change your entire career based on what you read here. Let's start by briefly looking at what Photoshop is. In this chapter, we'll see how Photoshop fits into the bigger picture of digital art. I will also give you some hints as to what we'll cover throughout this book.

What Is Photoshop?

Photoshop is the world's leading image-editing program. All other imaging programs combined aren't half as popular or powerful as Photoshop. People use Photoshop in everything from designing posters to designing fashions. They use it to edit pictures of people's grandkids and of supermodels. They use Photoshop in blockbuster Hollywood movies and in video games. Anything you can do with a photo, you can do in Photoshop. Whether you're reading this book for entertainment, profit, or both, you'll be happy to know that using Photoshop is fun, and that Photoshop is going to be around for a very long time.

 The term "image" is used to refer to digital photos, digital art, or anything else you happen to be working on in Photoshop.

What You Can Do with Photoshop

In the early days of Photoshop (that is, the 1990s), Photoshop
was primarily a photo editing tool. Photoshop has developed and
progressed into something much more. Photoshop 6 introduced
cleaner text for printing. Photoshop 7 introduced some very
robust painting tools. As we'll see later in this chapter, the
last few versions of Photoshop have allowed you to create,
import, and manipulate 3D objects, create animation, edit video,
organize your photo library, and create media for cell phones.

Figure 1-1 shows an example of what can be done in
Photoshop. I was playing around with this photo of my wife. I
love being able to take a photo and create a piece of art with it.
The best part is that I haven't altered the image permanently in
any way. I can go back and remove the green flowers next to
her eyes, or change the background colors, or whatever else I
want to do. In this book, you'll see how to work with objects in
Photoshop in such a way that you can always make changes later.

FIGURE 1-1 An artistic experiment
with Photoshop

One of the great aspects of Photoshop that we will be constantly looking at in this book is the ability to use layers. Layers didn't exist when Photoshop was first released; all painting, color correction, and effects took place on a single layer. This was just like painting on a canvas. If you messed up, your only choice was to paint over the mistake or start over. But with the introduction of layers, you could start putting pieces of your work onto separate parts of your image. These separate parts (layers) can be moved, resized, colored, and otherwise adjusted independently of all other pieces of your work in Photoshop.

Figure 1-2 shows a faux side view of the layers that comprise this project. Notice that most of the layers do not take up the entire document as the background does. Because these elements are all on separate layers, I can adjust each one without affecting the others. We'll be talking a great deal about layers as we go along.

FIGURE 1-2 The layers that make up the image seen in Figure 1-1

The World of Photoshop

As mentioned, the world of Photoshop is now a pretty big world. You probably will want to use other creative programs in harmony with Photoshop. If that's the case, you'll be glad to know that because of Photoshop's standing in the industry, many programs can recognize files in the PSD format, which is Photoshop's native file type. Here's a short list of the more common applications that can use PSD files:

- **Adobe Flash** The standard for web animation, web video, and web interactivity.
- **Adobe After Effects** The standard for video effects and motion graphics.
- **Adobe Encore** Adobe's DVD authoring program. Encore can automatically create DVD menus from PSD files.
- **Adobe Illustrator** The standard for vector graphics, logo creation, and digital drawing.
- **Adobe InDesign** The standard for page design (also called "page layout").
- **Adobe Premiere Pro** Adobe's video editing program.
- **Apple Final Cut Pro** One of the world's most popular video-editing programs.
- **Autodesk Maya and 3DS Max** The world's most popular 3D applications.

But Wait, There's More

Photoshop now ships with additional programs. *Adobe Bridge* is a file browsing application that allows you to sort, organize, and rank images. You can also download images from your digital camera to your computer by using Bridge. Bridge can open images, group them, perform some Photoshop automation commands, and much more.

Device Central is another application that we'll look at later in this book (Chapter 15). It was specifically created for making content for cell phones and mobile devices. It contains profiles—with photos—of a huge library of cell phones. It can also instantly create Photoshop documents that match the exact specs of a particular phone.

Perhaps my favorite "bonus" application that comes with Photoshop is Adobe *Camera Raw*. Many higher-end digital cameras allow you to save photos in a raw file format. This is like a digital negative—completely unprocessed and pristine. Camera Raw is a plug-in application that works with these files to color correct and adjust them.

What's Coming Up

Most Photoshop books focus almost entirely on photos and image editing. But Photoshop isn't just for photographers anymore. Of course, we'll look a great deal at editing images. But we'll also learn a lot about design and color. Creativity will be a major focus of the entire book, and we'll look at painting, drawing, and special effects. We'll look at issues that web designers and those that work in video might encounter. This is an introductory Photoshop book that doesn't try to force you down the standard path.

We'll also start from the beginning. If software programs like Photoshop intimidate you, have no fear. In the next chapter, we'll start by looking at Photoshop's interface and getting familiar with how to maneuver through its panels and menus. Then, bit by bit, you'll continue to learn about Photoshop's main features, building as we go. I've even written an entire chapter devoted specifically to a new version of Photoshop, called Photoshop Extended, which allows support for 3D and video files. You'll also see how to get your work out of Photoshop so that it can be used by other programs, printed, or put on the Web or on a cell phone. We'll also devote an entire chapter to Photoshop's arsenal of automatic features. Why work when Photoshop can do it for you better and faster?

Finally, we'll finish this book by talking about something that it's tough to find information on. We'll see how to make a living using Photoshop. It may sound farfetched to you now, but a few hundred pages down the road, you might be more convinced.

So what are we waiting for? Let's jump in and get acquainted with Photoshop CS4!

2

Getting Efficient with the Workspace

How to...

- Understand the Photoshop interface
- Control panels
- Maximize "screen real estate"
- Customize the Photoshop interface
- Use workspaces
- Open and work with multiple documents

Now that we've looked at the overall Photoshop workflow, let's examine the workspace a little more closely. What better way to get acquainted with Photoshop than to know its interface? Most books and training about software programs begin with a tour of the interface, and that tour is typically skipped by most learners. Granted, learning about panels and menus is not the most exciting thing, but understanding the interface is a critical step in becoming a power user. Many self-taught users have a great deal of artistic skill, but find it difficult to become true professionals because they are inept at following workflow basics. Each tidbit of interface knowledge may seem small and insignificant on its own, but compounded they will allow you to produce your best work in the shortest time.

About Panels

The work area in Photoshop is largely made up of several task-centric, mini work areas called *panels*. Most workflows use the Layers panel most frequently. Panels can be contracted and expanded to allow you more room to work. When expanded, panels that have been grouped

How to. . .   Approach Learning the Interface

In many classes that I have taught on creative software applications, I often run into students so overwhelmed by the sight of the interface with all of its tools, panels, customization options, menus, and buttons that they just freeze in panic when the program launches. One student interrupted class every few minutes to ask what a particular button did.

Yes, learning the role of every single button and panel is a daunting challenge. The good news is that you don't have to master every nook and cranny of Photoshop. Instead of asking, "What does that button do?" ask yourself "What tools do I need to know to get the results I want?"

Look at it this way—you've eaten thousands of meals in your lifetime, yet you might not know exactly how the food you eat gets converted to energy. You may not know what the pancreas does, or where stomach acid comes from, or how water is absorbed. But you know enough about the process to put food in your mouth. Think of the Photoshop interface in that way. You don't have to know the function of every button in Photoshop, you just need to know what tools to use to create the results you're looking for. You can add to your knowledge as you practice. Also note that many Photoshop tools and features probably wouldn't be beneficial for your particular workflow at all, so you don't have to learn them.

together are tabbed (see Figure 2-1). When they're collapsed, you can view the panels as icons and names, or just as icons, as shown in the accompanying illustrations. It's probably best to stick to the icons-and-names view until you can readily identify panels by their icons only.

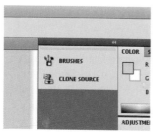

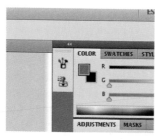

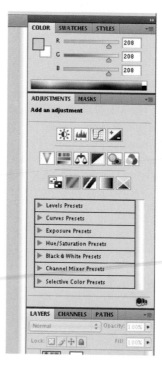

When the panels are collapsed in either the icon-and-name view or in the icon-only view, you can see the full-size panel as a pop-out by simply clicking the icon. Click the icon again to return the panel to its collapsed state. You can also collapse the

FIGURE 2-1 Each tab represents a different panel, and panels are grouped together.

How to. . .   Get Panels to Close Automatically

By default, panels opened from the icon view will stay open (popped out) even when you go back to your document and start working. However, you might find yourself wanting panels, like unwanted houseguests, to just disappear so you can get back to work. Thankfully, if you don't like the default behavior, you have a solution. You'll need to go to the Photoshop Preferences. On Windows, go to the Edit menu at the top of the screen, and choose Preferences | Interface. On a Mac OS, go to the Photoshop menu at the top of the screen, and choose Preferences | Interface. In this screen, select Auto-Collapse Iconic Panels, and then click OK to close the Preferences panel. Now you've changed the behavior of panels so that as soon as you start working, panels that have been opened from the icon view will automatically collapse.

FIGURE 2-2 Click the arrows on the upper-right of the panel to collapse the panel.

FIGURE 2-3 The Clone Source and the Brushes panels are grouped together when collapsed into icons (left) and are also grouped together as tabs when expanded (right).

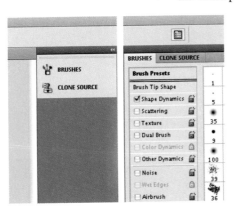

panel again by clicking the two right arrows on the upper-right of the panel (see Figure 2-2).

When you're viewing collapsed panels, the icons are grouped together in the same way the panels are grouped together. For example, the icons for the Clone Source panel and the Brushes panel are grouped together by default. After you open one of the panels by clicking on its icon, you'll see that these two panels are also grouped together when expanded (see Figure 2-3).

The Tools Panel

The Tools panel is the tall, skinny panel on the left side of the interface (see Figure 2-4). Even though it is called a panel, the Tools panel is in a class all its own. The Tools panel is where you go to get (surprise!) tools. For a certain task, how do you know whether you need to look for a tool or for a particular panel? Tools typically require you to manually adjust something in your document. So you would go to the Tools panel for tasks typically performed with your mouse such as drawing, selecting specific areas for editing, and painting. For example, if you wanted to paint a self-portrait, you would search for a tool (the Brush tool) in the Tools panel, not in one of the other panels. Other panels usually tweak the entire document at once when they make adjustments.

Screen Real Estate

The area of the screen that you work in is often called your *screen real estate*. By collapsing panels and using the interface efficiently, you will create more usable screen real estate. If your computer's video card supports it, you can hook up an additional monitor and store panels there as well. That will leave you a much larger portion of the screen to work on your documents.

 In the olden days of Photoshop, the Tools panel was shorter and was two columns wide (as opposed to the current default single-column view). If you'd like to make your Tools panel a little shorter and wider, you can click the upper-right arrows of the Tools panel to expand it.

If you are curious about learning other Adobe software programs, you'll find that Adobe has made it easier on you. The interfaces of most Adobe design programs—from Illustrator to InDesign to Flash to After Effects—have a great deal in common. These programs all share a customizable, docked, panel-based workspace, which is remarkably similar to what you see in Photoshop.

Other Key Interface Elements

Before we move on to customizing the Photoshop work area, let's get familiar with the other components of the interface, as shown in Figure 2-5.

The Menu Bar

At the very top of the interface, we have the Menu bar. As we go through this book, when I instruct you to go to a particular menu (for example, the Filter menu), this bar is where you would find the menu. These menus are great, especially when you're first learning Photoshop. For example, as you are working with layers, you may get stumped when trying to perform a certain function. Chances are, you can click the Layer menu and find what you're looking for.

Figure 2-4 The Tools panel

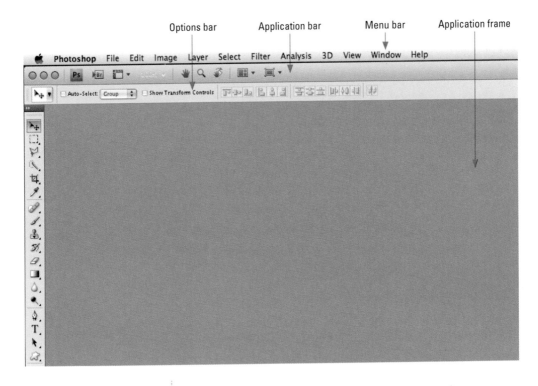

FIGURE 2-5 Key interface elements

 Each panel also has its own menu, called a "fly-out" menu, or a panel menu. The icon is on the upper right of every panel and looks like four horizontal lines with a down arrow on the left side of them. Thus, the Layer menu is at the top of the interface, while the Layers panel menu is in the Layers panel.

The Application Bar

Immediately below the Menu bar, we find the Application bar. This is new to the CS4 version of Photoshop. This area is a convenient place to access commonly used features and tools. From the Application bar, you can launch Adobe's file-browsing application, *Bridge.* You can also select the Hand tool to view a different area of an image, or the Zoom tool to zoom into or out of an image. Later in this book, we'll cover more of the features available in the Application bar.

For this book, I'll be using Photoshop on a Mac computer. On Windows computers, the Application bar may be in a different location. Don't worry; everything still works the same. The differences are only cosmetic.

The Options Bar

Below the Application bar is the Options bar. This area is *context sensitive*, meaning that it gives you options for the tool that is currently selected. I find it very helpful. Photoshop tools are great, but they often need to be fine-tuned and tweaked before they deliver the results you're looking for. The Options bar is the headquarters for such adjusting.

 The term "context sensitive" is used often in technical documentation for software programs. Basically, it's a geek's way of saying "it changes based on what you have selected." If you have one of the type tools selected, you'll be able to use the Options bar to adjust the font, font size, and so forth. If you select the Brush tool, the text options will disappear, and the Options bar will change to allow you to select different brushes.

The Application Frame

Along with the Application bar, the Application frame is a new feature of the CS4 version of Photoshop. The Application frame is essentially just the gray background in Photoshop. This mostly affects Mac users. Previous versions of Photoshop on the Mac had no application background, allowing you to see through to your desktop. If you are a Mac user and you want your Photoshop to look like it did in previous versions, simply go to the Window menu and deselect Application Frame.

While many Mac users prefer to see their desktop in Photoshop so that it's a little easier to grab documents and drop them into Photoshop, I actually prefer the new behavior. It's much cleaner than seeing Photoshop and your desktop; I don't find myself accidentally selecting the desktop (and thereby deselecting Photoshop) as I did before on the Mac; the desktop colors don't throw me off when I'm performing color adjustments; and also we Mac users now get a great Photoshop feature that Windows users have had for years.

On Windows, or now on a Mac with the Application frame visible, you can simply double-click anywhere in the blank gray background to open a file (see Figure 2-6). This is a great shortcut to the other methods of opening a file. Note that this only works for the first image you open. After that, you'll need to open images by going to the File menu or by using the shortcut.

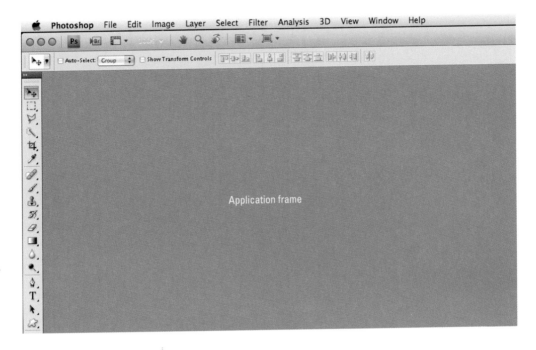

FIGURE 2-6 Double-click anywhere in the Application frame to open a file.

Customizing

One of the best aspects of the Photoshop interface is that you can customize it. You can move panels around, get rid of the panels you don't want, create "floating" panels, retrieve panels that are missing from your current interface layout, and save custom workspaces based on different tasks.

Moving Panels Around

Photoshop does a great job of guessing the way you'd like to have your panels grouped together. But its psychic abilities can go only so far; it really pays to be able to move panels around so that the interface can help you work as efficiently as possible.

To move a panel, simply drag the name of the panel (the panel's tab) to another group. Let's practice with the Styles panel. If the Styles panel is not open, any other panel will make a fine substitute. First, click the tab for the Styles panel, and then drag it to another group of panels. Once you see the blue highlight

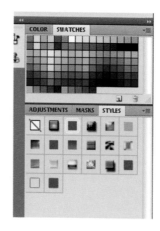

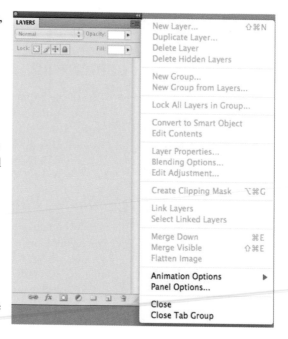

FIGURE 2-8 After moving the Styles panel to a new group of panels

FIGURE 2-7 The blue highlight indicates the new destination for the panel being moved.

around the destination group (see Figure 2-7), release the mouse; the panel has found a new home (see Figure 2-8).

Closing Unwanted Panels

Most of the panels that you see when you first open Photoshop are panels that you will hardly ever use. Why have them cluttering up your precious work area? Get rid of them! I'll show you how to get them back in a minute, so don't worry about hurting anything. To close panels, simply click the panel fly-out menu (see Figure 2-9) or right-click the name of the panel (that is, the tab). In both instances, a menu will pop up. Choose Close from that menu to hide that panel.

Fly-out menus are used to give you additional options for that panel. Thus, some panels (like the Navigator panel) don't have many options, while other panels (like the Layers panel) have a multitude of options.

FIGURE 2-9 The panel's fly-out menu

To get even more screen real estate without closing panels, simply double-click a panel's tab to vertically collapse it as well as all panels grouped with it. To restore the panel to the way it was, just double-click it again.

Creating "Floating" Panels

In the olden days of Photoshop, when Google was only a search engine and only one type of iPod existed, panels were called *palettes* and they weren't docked. They just kind of floated around in space. It was a mess. But if you want to undock your panels from the interface and have them "float" like they used to, simply drag the tab of a panel away from the other panels in the panel group. The panel will now hover over everything else (see Figure 2-10).

 To hide all open panels, press TAB on your keyboard. Press TAB again to get the panels back.

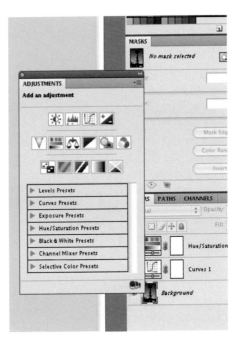

While I prefer the new system of docked panels, I often still find myself floating panels for certain tasks. For example, when I'm painting, I like to have the Brushes panel floating right next to where I'm painting. That way, when I'm ready to switch brushes or to edit them, I don't have to go far to get the tools for the job.

What happens when you want the floating panel to return to its default behavior as a docked panel? Simply drag it where you want it to go, just like the way you moved panels earlier in this section.

FIGURE 2-10 Dragging a panel's tab away from the panel group makes the panel float around instead of being grouped with other panels or docked to the interface.

If you ever want to reorder the tabs in a panel, just drag the panel's tab to the spot you want it. For example, if the tabs in your group are, from left to right, Layers, Channels, Paths, and you want the order to be Channels, Layers, Paths, then drag the tab for the Channels panel to the left so that it comes before the Layers panel.

Retrieving Missing Panels

If you need to work in a panel that you've closed, or if you need to access a panel that is not visible by default, all you have to do is select it from the Window menu at the top of the screen. From this menu, you will see a list of all of the panels available to you in Photoshop. As you can see in Figure 2-11, the menu has even more panels than the default workspace would lead you to believe. In the Window menu, when the name of a panel has a checkmark next to it, it indicates that panel is currently open in the interface.

 Most other Adobe applications have a Window menu that allows you to retrieve panels in the same way.

Working with Workspaces

If you work in an environment with many other people, perhaps you have experienced the unfortunate occasion of coming back from a vacation, only to find that fellow employees have worked on your machine and messed up your workspace. Maybe panels have been moved or rearranged, or keyboard shortcuts have been reassigned. Thankfully, Photoshop has the capability to save and access different interface configurations, called *workspaces.*

These workspaces can be used to accommodate additional users, or they can be used for specific tasks. Let's say, for example, that you are working with text, and then you plan to do some painting. These are two completely different tasks that use two completely different sets of panels. So, you could create one workspace that has what you need for text editing, and create another workspace that has what you need for painting. Taking advantage of workspaces in Photoshop may seem inconvenient at first, but it can make you much more efficient.

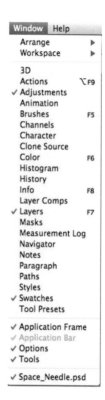

FIGURE 2-11 To open panels, go to the Window menu.

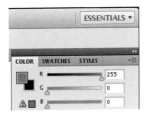

Using the Included Workspaces

Adobe has provided several workspaces that come with Photoshop. These can be accessed from the drop-down list on the far right end of the Application bar. The default workspace, shown here, is called Essentials.

Typically, these workspaces are used for specific workflows. For example, if you select the Painting workspace, the only panels that appear onscreen are panels that you would want for painting, such as the Brushes panel, the Color panel, the Swatches panel, and so on.

But these workspaces can also be helpful in other ways. In the last few versions of Photoshop, Adobe has provided a "what's new" workspace (see Figure 2-12). When this workspace is selected, your panels stay the same, but the menus change to highlight features of Photoshop that are either new or improved in the current version of Photoshop. For more information on changing menu colors, see the "The Secret Powers of Workspaces" sidebar.

FIGURE 2-12 When you select the What's New In CS4 workspace, features that are new or revised are marked in blue.

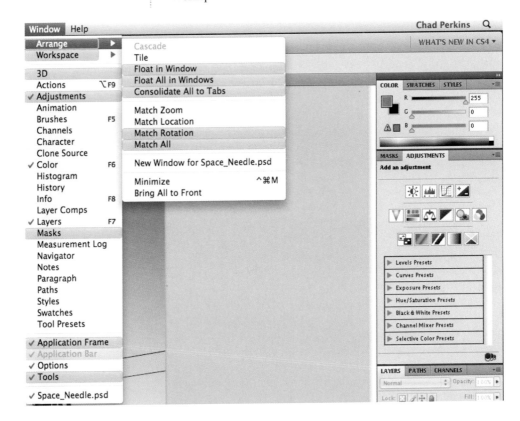

The Secret Powers of Workspaces

Not only can workspaces store information about how you like your panels laid out and which ones you want visible or hidden, but also panels can store customized menu settings and keyboard shortcuts.

If you go to the Edit menu, you can choose either Keyboard Shortcuts or Menus. If you select Keyboard Shortcuts, a dialog box will pop up allowing you to customize keyboard shortcuts. If you find yourself constantly using a particular function in Photoshop, in most cases you can create a keyboard shortcut for it. You can also change the keyboard shortcut if one already exists for it.

If you select Edit | Menus, you will have two main choices to customize menus. You can click the eye icon next to a menu item in a given menu to hide that option. For example, if you know that you'll never use a certain command, why have it take up space in a menu? Few if any users of Photoshop use every function and command. You don't need any visual speed bumps as you navigate Photoshop's interface looking for ways to make your art, so why not get them out of the way?

You can also customize menu items by making them a different color so that they stand out. That way, when you open a menu, your eye will instantly be drawn to the functions that you use most. Or, if you wear several hats (perhaps you create paintings, edit photos, and then post them to a web site), you can color menu items based on different workflows. The menu items you use for painting might be yellow, menu items you use for editing photos might be red, and so on.

Workspaces let you save panel locations, keyboard shortcuts, and menus. But you don't have to save all three. You can pick and choose which are saved in your workspace. The What's New In CS4 workspace, for example, does not change your panel locations or your keyboard shortcuts, only your menus.

Creating Your Own Workspaces

Now that you know how cool workspaces are, we'll talk about how to create them. It couldn't be easier. All you have to do is set up your panels, menus, and/or keyboard shortcuts the way you want them; then go to the workspace drop-down list and select Save Workspace. You will get a simple dialog box asking both the name of your new workspace and which components of the workspace (for example, panel locations, menus, keyboard shortcuts) you wish to save as part of the workspace. Once you click OK, your custom workspace will show up in the Workspace drop-down list with all of the others.

Working with Documents

Now that we know our way around, it's time to import an image and to get the hang of navigating around documents. This is even more critical to your workflow than getting acquainted with interface elements. Even if you already know a thing or two about Photoshop, the next few sections will cover impressive new features and some lifesaving shortcuts.

Opening Documents

First, we need to bring an image into Photoshop. This action is called *opening* in Photoshop, although in other applications it might be called "importing" or something similar. In Photoshop, the terms are essentially synonymous.

 As with several commands in Photoshop, you have many ways to do the same thing. This can be intimidating at first because it seems overwhelming to learn everything. The good news is that you don't have to learn it all. You only need to learn and use the way that you like best.

To open a file, choose File | Open. Alternatively, you could use the keyboard shortcut, CTRL-O (Windows)/CMD-O (Mac). As mentioned before, you can also use my preferred method to open files by double-clicking the Application frame, assuming it's visible. For this chapter, you can open one of your own images, or just follow along.

Tabbed Documents

Another very welcome new feature in Photoshop CS4 is the tabbed documents feature. Similar to what you might find in your web browser when you have multiple web pages open in the same window, Photoshop groups documents into tabs when more than one file is open at a time:

To cycle through open documents, use the keyboard shortcut CTRL-TAB (for both platforms).

Navigating Documents

Once you have a document (or documents) open, it's important that you're able to navigate it well. By *navigate* I'm referring to zooming in, zooming out, and panning around. Again, you'll find numerous ways to do this as well.

The "Spacebar" Shortcuts

Not only are keyboard shortcuts my favorite way to navigate documents, but they are the *only* way I navigate documents in Photoshop. All three use the SPACEBAR, so I affectionately refer to them as the "spacebar" shortcuts.

To zoom into an image, hold down the CTRL key (Windows)/CMD key (Mac) and the SPACEBAR to temporarily access (aka "toggle") the Zoom tool. Then, while still holding those keys, simply click anywhere on the image to zoom into that area.

After zooming in a couple times, you'll want to know how to zoom back out again. To do this, you can simply replace CTRL/CMD with ALT/OPT (while still holding down the SPACEBAR, of course). As before, click with those keys held down to zoom out.

Once you are zoomed into your image close enough that you can see the scroll bars on the right side and/or on the bottom of your image, you can hold down only the SPACEBAR to toggle the Hand tool. Then, as you drag with the SPACEBAR held down, you'll move the image around. Actually, this doesn't move the image or change it in any way; it only changes your view of the image. Another way to think of this is that it moves the camera, not the actor.

New Tricks

I've been teaching these "spacebar" shortcuts for years. But the current version of Photoshop has actually added a little improvement. If your graphics card supports OpenGL, you can hold down CTRL/CMD and the SPACEBAR, and then click and hold down the mouse button. This will cause your image to zoom in until you release the mouse button. You've got to try this. It makes the image look like a rocket that's launching at your face, and the only way to stop sudden destruction is to release the mouse button.

The Magic of Navigating with Keyboard Shortcuts

The really cool thing about navigating documents with the keyboard shortcuts just mentioned is that they toggle only navigational tools. That means that as soon as you let go of the keys on your keyboard—often called *modifier keys*—Photoshop automatically switches back to whatever tool you were using before pressing the modifier keys!

Let's say that you're painting with the Brush tool in a Photoshop document. Using any other navigation method, you would need to move your cursor to change the view of the document, and perhaps go back and select the Brush tool again after that. Who has the time and patience to do that? Instead, we use these trusty keyboard shortcuts, and when we release them, we're back to our Brush tool and can continue painting.

Although this is absolutely the most efficient way to get around an image in Photoshop, it isn't the only way. Maybe you're using Photoshop just for fun, not to make money, and speed isn't a consideration. That's okay, too. Other methods to navigate don't require so much memorization (or finger dexterity).

The Navigator Panel

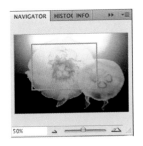

The Navigator panel is another way that you can navigate documents (see Figure 2-13). As you drag the slider at the bottom of the Navigator panel to the right, you zoom into the image. Dragging to the left zooms back out. Once you zoom in, a little red rectangle on the image preview in the Navigator panel appears, representing the portion of the image you are now seeing in the main document window. You can drag that rectangle around to see different portions of your image, which is similar to what you saw previously with the Hand tool.

In the bottom left corner of the Navigator panel, you can also type in a specific zoom percentage. This is helpful for those times when you've been zooming in or out a lot, and you want to see your image at an exact magnification, such as 100%.

FIGURE 2-13 Zooming with the Navigator panel

As with all other panels in Photoshop, if the Navigator panel is not visible, you can select it from the Window menu at the top of the interface to reveal it in all of its navigational glory.

Tools

Instead of using keyboard shortcuts to toggle navigational tools, you can select them from the Tools panel on the left side of the interface.

You can select the Zoom tool (which looks like a magnifying glass, shown next) to zoom in and out. Once you select the tool from the bottom of the Tools panel, click to zoom in, or hold down ALT (Windows)/OPT (Mac) while clicking to zoom out.

To change the view of your image, you can select the Hand tool in the Tools panel, right above the Zoom tool. Once you select the tool, simply drag your image around to change your view.

The Application Bar

Mentioned briefly earlier in this chapter, the Application bar is a new feature that provides quick access to commonly used tools. It's no surprise, then, that you can also find a Hand tool and a Zoom tool at the top of the interface in the Application bar as shown here.

 Also in the Application bar, right next to the Hand and Zoom tools, you'll find a new tool in Photoshop CS4 called the Rotate View tool. This is used for temporarily rotating your image. As with the Hand tool, this only changes your view, not the image itself.

Keyboard Shortcuts List

Hopefully by now I've convinced you of the power of keyboard shortcuts. When teaching classes, I'm often asked where to find a list of all keyboard shortcuts. In previous versions of Photoshop, you might find enclosed in the package a sheet listing all shortcuts. But this list is absent from recent versions. A few versions ago, Photoshop introduced the ability to customize keyboard shortcuts. Instructions on how to do that were provided earlier in this chapter. However, by going to Edit | Keyboard Shortcuts, you can get a list of all keyboard shortcuts in addition to customizing them. So, even though this option was not intended to be a reference, it's a handy list of shortcuts.

Be aware that not all keyboard shortcuts will be on this list. Many keyboard shortcuts are "hidden" shortcuts. For example, you probably won't find the "spacebar" shortcuts on that list, but that's okay. As you go through this book, I'll provide some of the most important keyboard shortcuts as we need them.

3

Document and Layer Basics

How to...

- Create a new Photoshop document
- Understand resolution
- Understand color modes
- Work with layers
- Blend layers together

We've just looked at the face of Photoshop—the *inter*face to be exact. It's now time to get to know it a little better. The bulk of our study in this chapter will be about layers. Layers are perhaps the most critical element of Photoshop and can greatly increase your efficiency and the quality of your final product. Your ability to use Photoshop well will largely depend upon your ability to use layers well.

But first we'll look at what makes up a document—resolution, size, pixels, and more. This information is a little intense, but it's the kind of thing that can save your sanity (and your reputation with clients) if you're in the know.

Creating a New Photoshop Document

You have two ways to use Photoshop—one is to start with images that you've imported (like we did in Chapter 2); the other is to start with a document that you've created from scratch in Photoshop. I usually like to start my projects, especially artistic projects, with a brand-new document. This way I can ensure that my document is set up to the correct specs for output. If you start with an existing project that is too small, it might be impossible later to make it large enough to print. If you begin with a document that is too large, it will slow you down unnecessarily as you're working.

What we'll do now is create a document from scratch. To create a new document, you can click the Create A New Document button on the Welcome screen. Or, if you're like me and you just close that semi-annoying screen without even looking at it carefully, you can create a new document by going to the Menu bar at the top of the interface, and choosing File | New (see Figure 3-1).

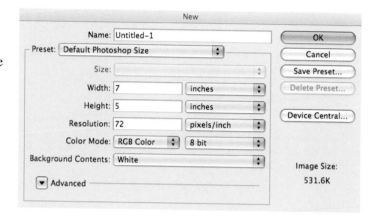

FIGURE 3-1 The New dialog box

  You can also create a new document at any time by using the easy-to-remember keyboard shortcut: CTRL (Windows)/CMD (Mac)-N (as in "N" for "New").

At first this dialog box can be intimidating as you glance around at all the empty fields. Don't worry, I'll tell you what you need to know to get started. And Photoshop also has your back. Photoshop understands that this is a little overwhelming to new users. It also knows that even if you are a total pro and know exactly what you should put in every field, it gets tedious filling out all this technical info. So what's Photoshop's solution?

Document Presets

Photoshop has created a plethora of presets for you to choose from when creating documents. These presets are nicely arranged into a variety of categories based on different workflows. Figure 3-2 shows the drop-down list of presets. This list might open your eyes

FIGURE 3-2 The list of document presets

to how many industries depend on the features of Photoshop to get the job done. People in the video world, web graphic designers, print graphic designers, those who create content for mobile phones and portable devices, those in the film industry, photographers, and many more use Photoshop on a daily basis. And for each of them, Photoshop has document presets ready to get them started.

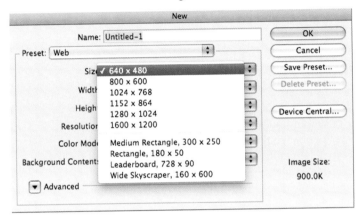

Each preset also has a variety of sizes to choose from that are common to that medium or industry. For example, if you were to select the Web preset and then click the Size drop-down list, you would be presented with most common computer screen resolutions, as well as some sizes useful for web graphics.

If you were to change the preset to Film & Video, and then click the Size drop-down list again, you would see an entirely different list of sizes to choose from.

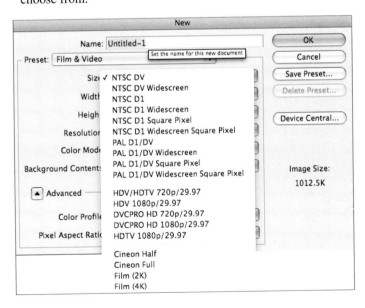

For now, go ahead and select the Photo preset if you're following along. Next, we'll talk about the components that make up this preset, and indeed, the entire document.

 You can change the unit of measurement to a variety of units. The default unit of measurement in the United States is inches. For web and video documents, inches are irrelevant. By clicking the word "inches," you access a drop-down list from which you can change the unit of measurement to pixels, centimeters, picas, and more.

The Truth about Resolution

The term *resolution* is tossed around a lot these days. The problem is that it can mean so many different things, depending on the circumstances in which it's used. In some circles, the phrase "low res" (short for "low resolution") has come to refer to an image's quality. It's very important to know that Photoshop (and most professionals) never equate resolution with quality. It is quite possible to have an image that is high resolution, but is still low quality.

What Are Pixels?

When Photoshop refers to resolution, it refers to how many pixels are in a given area. So, before we understand resolution, we need to learn a little about pixels. The term *pixel* is short for "picture element." Pixels are the tiny squares that make up images on a computer. Even when you're looking at a photo of

 **Did You Know?**   **Name Your Stuff!**

Even though we're not going to spend much time in this chapter naming documents, I strongly recommend that you name your document while you're creating it. Naming files, layers, and anything else you can in Photoshop might be a slight inconvenience initially, but it's well worth it in the long run. Otherwise, after you have about 30 Photoshop documents on your computer that are only named with variations of "Untitled-#," you will be driven mad. Better to accept the fact that naming files and layers is just a part of life, and name your Photoshop documents.

donuts and wheels arranged in a circle, it's all just made with squares! Check out Figure 3-3, where I've zoomed into an image close enough to be able to see them.

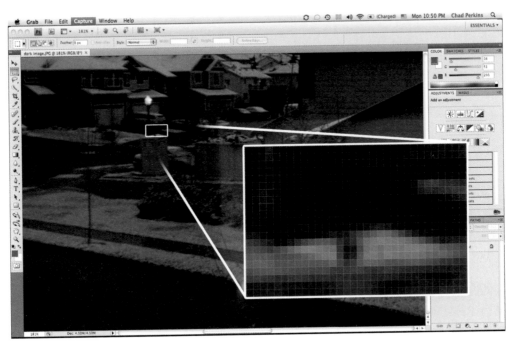

FIGURE 3-3 These squares, called "pixels," are the building blocks of images.

The number of pixels that occupy a particular area determine the resolution. The fewer pixels in a given area (like a square inch), the more blocky the area will appear, and the lower the resolution. When there are more pixels in an image, they will be smaller and less conspicuous, and the resolution will be higher.

Ppi, Dpi, and Lpi

To add to the confusion about the true definition of the word "resolution," even the graphics community can't get their facts straight half the time. Resolution on a computer screen is expressed in pixels per inch (*ppi*). This is because computer monitors have pixels. Printers and scanners often print and scan using dots or lines. When we refer to the resolution of these and other such devices, we use the terms *dpi* (dots per inch) and *lpi* (lines per inch). People often mistakenly use the terms dpi and lpi when referring to computer files, even though computer screens have neither dots nor inches.

Technically, computer monitors do have "dots," as each pixel is made up of three color "dots"—one each of red, green, and blue. However, most monitor specs read in terms of pixel dimensions, not dot dimensions. (But you can often find manufacturers mistakenly labeling monitors in terms of dpi when they're actually referring to ppi.)

The Bottom Line (per Inch)

You must keep in mind resolution when you are creating your documents in Photoshop. Just because you tell Photoshop that you want to create a document that is 8.5×11 inches doesn't necessarily mean that you've set up your document properly. How many pixels are in those inches? For onscreen graphics and images, or for images intended for video or 3D programs, 72 ppi is the standard, because that is the resolution of computer monitors and TV screens.

Printed documents require smaller pixels to look clean, so the standard is usually about 300 ppi. Before printing big jobs (that is, pretty much anything you're not printing from a desktop inkjet printer), be sure to ask your print provider how many pixels per inch your document should be in order to look correct when printed on their machines. Even though 300 ppi is a fairly common standard, you should never assume anything. I once designed a CD cover for an independent punk band, and I assumed that 300 ppi would be fine. However, their CD production house recommended I create the art at 600 ppi—twice the resolution that I was planning on.

When asking your printing agency about resolution, be sure that you get the resolution for your computer document, *not* the resolution of their printer. The first person you ask about this may not know the correct answer. What they might be tempted to tell you is the resolution of their printer, which may be something like 133 lpi. In most cases, this does not translate to document resolution.

Document Color

The rest of the fields used to create a basic document pertain to color. We'll save an in-depth discussion about this foundational topic for the next chapter. For now, you've just got to know a couple of things before creating a new document.

Color Mode

Color mode refers to the way a document "understands" color. The two most common document color modes are RGB and CMYK. These abbreviations stand for Red, Green, Blue, and Cyan, Magenta, Yellow, and Black, respectively.

Intro to RGB   Red, green, and blue are the color components of light. As such, you should use this color mode when using Photoshop to create images for 3D programs, video games, motion graphics, web graphics, or anything that will have its final output on a computer monitor or TV screen.

Intro to CMYK   In the same way that the RGB model is what light is made up of, CMYK basically contains the opposite colors. I'll explain this in greater detail in the next chapter, but what you need to know now is that CMYK is used as the color model for ink. Use this color model for most jobs that will be commercially printed.

Color Depth

This is a huge can of worms. Until you get more proficient at Photoshop, leave this setting at 8 bit. In a nutshell, this refers to the number of possible colors. A 2-bit image would contain only four colors. An 8-bit image can contain 16.7 million colors. Scientists estimate that the human eye can perceive about 10 million colors. So, for now, 8 bit will be fine.

Background Color

Ah, finally some respite from the mentally intensive properties used to create a new Photoshop document. The Background Content drop-down list shown here essentially allows you to specify a background color for your document while you are creating it. From this list, you can choose to create a White background layer, a Background Color that is the same color as the current background color in the Tools panel, or simply to create a Transparent background layer.

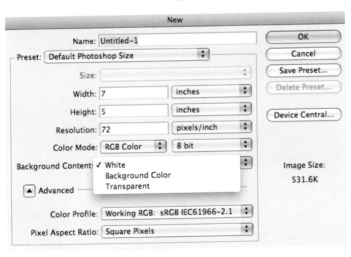

The ability to change your background color

here really isn't a big deal. It's just about as easy to change the background color later as it is to change the color of the background layer here. Now we're ready to look more closely at layers.

Introduction to Layers

As previously mentioned, layers are an integral part of using Photoshop effectively. They basically contain the various pieces of our documents. Think of the layers of a sandwich. If someone puts a layer of bacon on your sandwich, and you don't want it, you can easily remove it. There's some flexibility there. But what if you wanted to remove the lactose from the Swiss cheese? That's not quite so easy, because the lactose is a component of the Swiss cheese. In Photoshop terms, we would say that they are on the same layer.

Analogies aside, let's say you have a photo of some friends, and you want to add some artistic brushstrokes to the photo. If you add the paint strokes onto the same layer with the photo, and then you want to make changes later (move them, recolor them, change their transparency, and so on), you would be in trouble. It would be extremely difficult, and in some cases impossible. Not to mention that the pixels that you painted over would also be ruined and would need to be repaired, which would probably take half an eternity.

On the other hand, if you create a new, blank layer and then paint on that, it would be extremely simple to adjust the paint stroke. And painting on a new, separate layer would have the added benefit of leaving the pixels of your photo untouched.

For the next example, I'll use a Photoshop document I created from scratch using the New dialog box.

The Layers Panel

The Layers panel is really the hub of our layers-centric workflow. Figure 3-4 shows the Layers panel in all of its layered glory. If your Layers panel is not visible, you can retrieve it from the Window menu at the top of the interface.

FIGURE 3-4 The Layers panel

From the Layers panel, we can select our layers, create new ones, reorder layers, blend them together, create masks to temporarily hide portions of a layer, group layers, and performs many other tasks as well. Notice in Figure 3-4 that when you create a new document, a background layer is already created for you. For more info on the background layer, check out the "Fiddle with the Background Layer" sidebar.

Note Photoshop actually offers several different types of layers: plain old layers, background layers, adjustment layers, text layers, smart object layers, and others. If you have Photoshop Extended, you can also have 3D or video layers.

 **Fiddle with the Background Layer**

By default, when you open a file or create a new document in Photoshop, it automatically creates a background layer for you. You can easily identify background layers because their name ("Background") appears in *italics,* and a little padlock appears to the right of its name.

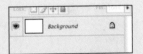

This layer is locked to prevent you from accidentally performing certain changes to it, such as moving the layer or rearranging its layer order in the Layers panel. If the background layer is really important to you, but you still want to play around with it, I recommend duplicating it by pressing CTRL (Windows)/CMD (Mac)-J after selecting the layer. Then you can edit the duplicate to your heart's content, and your original is left intact.

In some instances you might want to edit your background layer directly (not edit a copy). If you are exporting to another program or to video or 3D work, you may want transparent areas in your background layer, so that other objects may show through beneath the layers in the Photoshop document. Of course, if your background layer is transparent, you won't have to worry about that.

For whatever reason, if you want to unlock your background layer, simply double-click it. A dialog box will pop up asking you for the name of the layer and for a few other properties of the layer. The new default name is Layer 0, as shown here. You are then free to use the layer as you please.

Making New Layers

If you want to create a new layer, simply click
the Create A New Layer button at the bottom
of the Layers panel. The icon looks like a
notebook page about to be turned.

 The page-turning icon used to create a new layer can be seen throughout Photoshop and in almost all
Adobe applications. It is a universal icon indicating that something new will be created. Remember
this if you ever get stumped. If you're in the Swatches panel in Photoshop (or Adobe Illustrator) and
you want to create a new swatch, just click the page-turning icon. This works if you want to create a new brush
in the Brushes panel, a new style in the Styles panel, a 3D light in the 3D panel, and so on.

The Layers panel will then show you that a new layer has
been created. Photoshop automatically names it Layer 1. If you
create another new layer (which you can do by using the same
method), the default name will be Layer 2, and so on. If you
hold down the ALT (Windows)/OPT (Mac) key while clicking
the Create A New Layer button, you can name the layer while
you're creating it. Or if the layer is already created, you can
rename it by double-clicking exactly the name of the layer and
typing the new name. It's important that you not double-click
to the left or right of the name of the layer because hidden
functions reside there. We'll talk about all that supersecret
Photoshop ninja stuff later.

 How many layers can you have in one document? As many as your computer can handle. So,
don't be conservative on layer creation unless you have a superhuge document or a superslow
computer.

What Is That Checkerboard Pattern?

You may have noticed that Photoshop shows
you a little "thumbnail," or preview, of the
contents of each layer. You can find the tiny
preview to the left of the name of each layer, as
shown in Figure 3-5.

FIGURE 3-5 Layer thumbnails in
the Layers panel

But with the new layer that was created, you may
have noticed that the layer thumbnail is a gray-and-white
checkerboard pattern. What gives? That's actually a familiar
Photoshop entity called the *transparency grid,* and you will
come to know it well as you gain experience in Photoshop.
It basically tells you that nothing is there. Before you go off
believing that Photoshop is simply crying wolf, I should point

out that the ability to view the transparent areas of a document is very helpful, as we'll soon see.

When you take your Photoshop documents to other applications—such as Adobe Flash to be animated, or to Adobe InDesign to be put in a page layout, or to Adobe After Effects to be composited into a video—you'll often want a transparent background so that you can change the background in the new application. This also helps to give you an idea of where "holes" are on a particular layer.

Tip You can change the size of the layer thumbnail by going to the fly-out menu of the Layers panel and selecting Panel Options. From there, you can choose whether to make the thumbnail larger, smaller, or to hide the layer thumbnail entirely. Hiding the layer thumbnail can help speed things along if you have a really big project with a lot of layers, or if you are on a slow computer.

Mini Project: The Magic of Layers

Let's take a little break for a simple project so that you can see firsthand how powerful layers are. We'll start from scratch. If you haven't created a new document, go ahead and do that now. Just use the default Photoshop size from the Preset drop-down list, and make sure the Background

Contents drop-down list is set to White. Next, make a new layer by clicking the Create A New Layer button in the bottom right corner of the Layers panel. See Figure 3-6 to make sure you're on the same page as I am.

Next, go to the Tools panel on the left side of the interface, and click once on the leftmost color swatch toward the bottom of the Tools panel.

FIGURE 3-6 The Layers panel so far

Note These two color swatches are the foreground and background color swatches. We'll look more closely at these, as well as the Adobe Color Picker, in the next chapter.

After clicking on that color swatch, we will meet an important new friend called the Color Picker (see Figure 3-7). We'll talk more in depth about how to use this area in the next chapter. For now, just know that this is where we come to select colors for certain tasks such as painting. The Color Picker has two main areas of focus, and unfortunately, they're kind of out of order. In the center of the Color Picker, we have a tall, narrow bar from which to select the basic color. You can drag the little arrows on the hue slider vertically, or you can simply click the color to use. For this example, I'm going to click somewhere in the blue area.

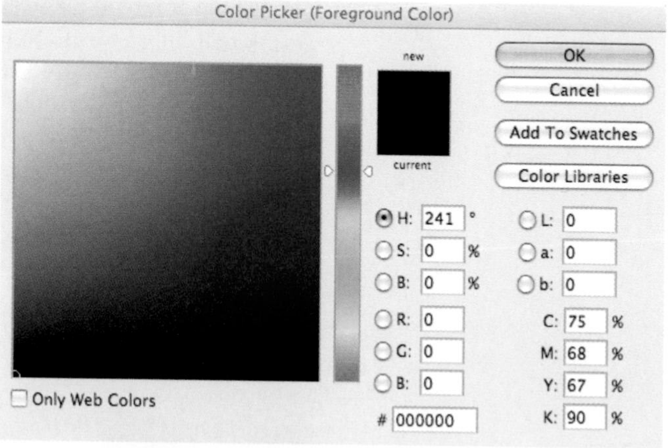

Next, we need to go to the big square on the left to fine-tune this blue color. Click in the upper-right corner of the square to select a bright, vibrant blue.

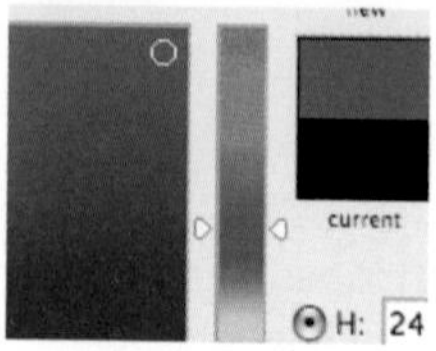

Click the OK button, or press ENTER (Windows)/RETURN (Mac) on your keyboard to accept the color and close the Color Picker. Now select the Brush tool by clicking it in the Tools panel, or by pressing B on your keyboard.

This turns your cursor into a paintbrush. We'll talk in more detail about the powerful painting tools in Photoshop in Chapter 5. For now, make sure that your new, blank layer is selected, and just drag in your document to paint a squiggle (see Figure 3-8). Isn't that fun?

FIGURE 3-7 Click the blue area in the hue slider to access blue colors.

FIGURE 3-8 The newly created blue paint squiggle. Notice that the paint squiggle is on the new blank layer we created, and not on the background layer.

Next, we'll re-create the last few steps. I'll go a little faster here, so if you're stumped on how to do something, just go back a few paragraphs to refresh your memory.

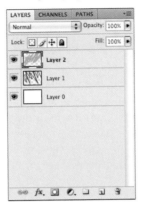

Create another new blank layer. Go back to the swatch in the Tools panel, and open the Color Picker again. This time, change the color in the narrow color bar from blue to green, and click OK to accept. Then draw a green paint squiggle on the new blank layer, making sure that some of the "paint" overlaps the corresponding area on the blue squiggle layer. When you're all done, your Layers panel should look like what's shown in Figure 3-9.

FIGURE 3-9 The Layers panel at this point

Notice what's going on here. The layer with the green squiggle is on top of the layer with the blue squiggle in the Layers panel. And it also covers up the blue squiggle. But we can change this through the magic of layers. If we later decide that we'd like to sandwich the green squiggle layer in between the blue squiggle layer and the white background, we can do so quickly and easily. Simply click the layer with the green squiggle, and then drag it down below the layer with the blue squiggle (see Figure 3-10). You've now rearranged your layers, which is something that would have been impossible to do if you had painted directly on the background layer.

FIGURE 3-10 The document after dragging the top layer (with the green paint) below the layer underneath it (the one with the blue paint)

Tip You might have noticed that it's already proving to be a challenge to keep track of layers with generic names. This would be a great time to rename them (discussed earlier in this chapter).

Another Project: Opacity and Layer Blending

Another one of the features of using layers is that we can blend them together in interesting ways. The most simple and speedy way to blend layers together is by using opacity. Opacity is the opposite of transparency. If something has an opacity value of 100%, that means it's completely visible. An opacity value of 0% indicates that an object is completely transparent.

Combining Images

Before we adjust opacity to blend layers together, we need to have layers to blend. So we'll now look at how to combine multiple images into the same Photoshop document.

Our first step is to open multiple images. I'll go to the File menu at the top left corner of the interface and choose Open. I will then open a file called *light image.jpg*. I will then repeat that process to open the file *dark image.jpg*. To follow along, open up a light image and a dark image from your image collection.

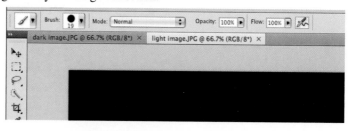

FIGURE 3-11 After you open multiple files, they show up as tabs in the Photoshop interface.

Or you can just read and watch me work some sweet image-editing magic on these pictures. When you open multiple files in Photoshop, Photoshop "stores" them in different windows. These are displayed as tabs toward the top of the interface (see Figure 3-11). Click one of the tabs to switch documents. This is one of the new, cool features in Photoshop CS4.

Tip You can switch between the two documents by using the keyboard shortcut CTRL-TAB (both platforms) and can close a document by clicking the little "x" next to the name of the document in the document's tab.

Now that we have both images open in separate documents, it's time to combine them into one document so that we can blend them together. You have a couple of ways to do this.

First, you can select one image and then copy and paste it onto the other one. In our example, we want to copy and paste the dark image on top of the light one. So, go to the dark image, and select the whole thing by pressing the keyboard shortcut CTRL (Windows)/CMD (Mac)-A.

Tip You can also select the entire image by going to the Select menu at the top and choosing All. You can also copy and paste by choosing those options from the Edit menu.

Then, with the dark image selected, press CTRL (Windows)/CMD (Mac)-C to copy the dark image. Then go over to the light image, and press CTRL (Windows)/CMD (Mac)-V to paste the dark image on top of the light image. When you've set it up correctly, your Layers panel should resemble the one in Figure 3-12.

Lowering the Opacity

Now we're ready to play with the opacity. You've probably noticed how the dark image completely obscured the light image. To blend these by lowering the opacity of the top layer, click and drag on the word Opacity in the Layers panel. Dragging to the left will reduce the opacity, while dragging to the right will increase it, up to 100%. I took the opacity of the top layer to 75%. Figure 3-13 shows what the project looks like now. Notice how the increased transparency of the dark image layer allows some of the light image beneath it to show through.

FIGURE 3-12 The Layers panel after combining the images

Tip If you know the exact amount of opacity you'd like to use, you can either double-click the numeric opacity field in the Layers panel, or you can drag to select the numbers; then type in the desired opacity percentage.

You can create a completely different effect by taking down the opacity even further. The result of taking the top layer's opacity down to 25% is shown in Figure 3-14. This allows for even more of the light image beneath to show through. The final result looks like the house is surrounded by early morning fog. Also, there's some guy taking a picture of it for some reason. Creepy.

FIGURE 3-13 The project with the top layer (the dark image) at 75% opacity

FIGURE 3-14 The project with the top layer at 25% opacity

4

Working with Color

How to...

- Understand color basics
- Use color to evoke emotional responses
- Tint an image
- Use color in different output media
- Use color swatches
- Use the Eyedropper tool

Color is perhaps the most important aspect of working with photos or art of any kind. Even if your only mission in Photoshop is to remove blemishes (or annoying people) from photographs, all photos essentially consist of variations in color. Colors also have strange powers, with each color evoking different emotional responses. In this chapter, we'll talk about some of those artsy-fartsy color basics, as well as how color is used in different media (such as printing, on the Web, and in video), and a few different ways to utilize colors in Photoshop.

Just realize going into this chapter that it might feel a little incomplete. Entire books have been written on most of the following subjects. I cover here only what you need to know to get started with Photoshop.

The Essentials of Color

Before we get into how to use color in Photoshop, we first need to look at what makes up a color. We'll also look at the emotional effects of color, and look a little at using colors together.

Hue, Saturation, and Lightness

As we'll see in this chapter, you can look at color in many different ways. One color model that has always made sense to me is that of hue, saturation, and lightness. We see this model often in Photoshop as well. These three properties refer to different elements of a color. It helps to know what these properties do so that when you want to turn a dark brown into a bright, vibrant blue, you'll know which properties you need to adjust.

 You can choose among several ways of looking at color, and great variations in terminology exist. The knowledge presented here will help you most while you're working with Photoshop.

What Is Hue?

Hue is what most people probably think of when they think of color. Hue essentially describes the color "family," such as reds, blues, greens, and so on. So, even though red and pink are different colors, they still share the same hue. If you had a photograph and you wanted to change the color of someone's shirt, more than likely you would only want to change the hue. Remember that "color" is really a combination of all of these attributes: hue, saturation, and lightness.

 An image adjustment in Photoshop called Hue/Saturation is one of my favorites. It uses the hue, saturation, and lightness model to adjust colors. We'll look at it in depth later in the book.

FIGURE 4-1 Blue with a high level of saturation

What Is Saturation?

Saturation is the intensity of a color. As we increase saturation, colors become more vibrant and intense. As we desaturate colors, they become faded and washed out. Completely desaturating a color will produce gray. Figures 4-1 and 4-2 show a blue color with different levels of saturation. Note that both of these blues have the same hue and lightness. The only thing that has changed is the saturation.

What Is Lightness?

Lightness is a self-explanatory color property. Increasing lightness makes a color lighter (closer to white), while decreasing lightness makes a color darker (closer to black).

FIGURE 4-2 The same color as in Figure 4-1, only desaturated

The Secret to Using Lightness

Although there really aren't any rules in working with hue and saturation, you should be aware of some rules when working with lightness. One of the most common tasks in any image editing program is to make things a little brighter. This is probably because people like to do supercool stuff at night, and also because it's often difficult to get enough light in a shot. But when you do brighten things a bit, don't neglect the shadows. In lower-budget image editing programs (and sometimes even in Photoshop), when you brighten an image, it universally brightens every pixel. So, as soon as you lighten an image even a little, you've lost pure black. The reverse is also true; when you darken every pixel in an image, you also darken the brightest pixel, completely losing pure white.

The moral: When you brighten images (or portions of them), make sure you're using effects that will allow your image to retain pure white and pure black. This will ensure a well-balanced image as far as tone is concerned, and it will keep you from looking like you don't know what you're doing (always a plus).

Figures 4-3 and 4-4 show the same blue from Figure 4-1 with varying amounts of lightness.

Tip Pastel colors are created by increasing lightness and decreasing saturation.

FIGURE 4-3 The blue swatch from Figure 4-1 with increased lightness

FIGURE 4-4 The blue swatch from Figure 4-1 with reduced lightness

The Emotional Effects of Color

When dealing with color, always keep in mind the way colors make people feel. I'm not suggesting that when people see red, they get mad. But when certain colors are used in certain ways, they do influence us.

Sound farfetched? How many times have you seen a blue "Stop" sign or a green "Danger" sign? Unless pranksters have been at work, I'm guessing you haven't seen one. It's because red has been shown to create feelings of caution and warning within us, so signs that try to get us to beware of danger are typically red.

Likewise, you've probably never seen an infomercial (or other televised sales pitch) that had a red background. In contrast to stop and danger signs, infomercials want your money, so they try to create feelings of reliability and stability. This is typically done with blue, as it radiates professionalism and trust.

FIGURE 4-5 Notice how the art looks a lot more intense when it uses warm tones.

Warm and Cool Colors

The two examples of the emotional effects of color we've looked at so far are red and blue. I used examples with these two colors intentionally, because they can evoke such powerful responses from people. In this section, we'll look at colors in terms of their temperature, such as "warm" and "cool" colors. Red and adjacent colors such as yellow and orange are referred to as warm tones. These are powerful colors that can create not only feelings of warning, but also passionate emotions such as anger or rage. See Figure 4-5 to see how warm colors can add to the intensity of art.

Or we can add just a little tint of these colors to create warmth instead of heat. If we have a photo, we can tint it with a warm color to add a little warmth. Notice how, in Figures 4-6 and 4-7,

FIGURE 4-6 The original image

33.33%   Doc: 7.13M/7.13M

33.33%   Doc: 7.13M/7.13M

FIGURE **4-7** The image with a warm tint to it

the image becomes much more endearing when warm colors are added. Hey, they don't call it heartwarming for nothing!

The use of tinted images, discussed in the "About Tinting" sidebar, is extremely common in the movies. Next time you're watching one, notice the colors of important scenes.

About Tinting

Like many concepts in the world of color, tinting can be confusing because the term is often used in different ways. In painting, a *tint* of a color means a color mixed with white to lighten the color, and a *shade* of a color is a color mixed with black to make it darker. Using this definition, pink is a tint of red.

But another definition of *tint* is more common in Photoshop, because it's more common in photography circles. Essentially, it means to subtly add a color to an entire image. This has an effect similar to using a colored filter on a camera lens. If you don't have experience with photography, it's like holding a piece of colored plastic-wrap over your lens. Perhaps the most common type of tinting is seen in sepia-toned images, which are photos that are black-and-white with a faint, dark yellow tint to them (think of the first part of the *Wizard of Oz*). This subtle addition of color to an entire image is the definition of tint that I will be using throughout this book unless otherwise specified. As we'll see in this chapter, tinting is a very powerful way of influencing the emotional message of an image.

Just as we've seen with warm colors, blue and its adjacent colors like purple and green are considered cool colors. Also, as with warm colors, how the temperatures make you feel is a good guide to how the colors should be used. Cool things like a breeze or ice cream are generally seen as calming and relaxing. But cold things can create feelings of alienation or fear. Cool colors work the same way. Used with restraint, cool colors create a relaxed feel. Used more intensely, they can create feelings of isolation. Figure 4-8 shows an image as is, and Figure 4-9 shows it tinted with cool colors. Does the image with the cool tint make you feel differently about it? What story does it tell that the original image does not?

Tip Because colder colors can create relaxed feelings, they are often the best choice for professional circumstances, like bank logos and the already-mentioned infomercials.

FIGURE 4-8 The original image

FIGURE **4-9** The image with a
cool tint

How to...   ## Examine Restaurant Logos

The use of colors in restaurant logos is a great way to study the effect that colors have on us. Notice that these logos are often the color of the foods that are served there. The logo colors of McDonald's remind me of fries and ketchup. It's no wonder we see similar color schemes in other fast-food hamburger chains, such as Wendy's, Burger King, Carl's Jr./Hardee's, and so on. Most foods have earth tones, so it makes sense that red, yellow, and orange are used so often. These colors are also mostly found in comfort foods, which is another reason for these businesses to use them in their logos.

Some restaurants want nothing to do with the greasy, unhealthy food served at these places. Instead they want to serve fresh food that caters to a more health-conscious audience. So what color would you guess they would use in their logo? If you said green, give yourself a wheatgrass smoothie, because you're right! It's a subtle touch, but Subway puts a green stroke (outline) around their logo, to imply that they are the healthier choice. Did you know that a small six-inch tuna sub from Subway has more calories (and fat) than a Quarter Pounder with Cheese at McDonald's? Subway's logo helps to convince eaters that it is always a healthier choice. It's amazing what a difference colors can make to a business and its identity.

Color in Context

The last touchy-feely thing I'll mention about colors is that everything has to be taken in context. It is possible to create really intense art that has blue in it. It's also possible to create art that creates feelings of isolation using yellow and orange. These are just general guidelines. But remember that they are guidelines because they resonate with human nature, not because some ancient nerd arbitrarily made this stuff up. So, while it is possible to create a feeling of calm with warm colors, it's a bit like tightening a screw with the backside of a hammer: the job can be done, but it's probably not the best tool for the job.

Using Colors Together

A friend and hero of mine, noted illustrator Bruce Heavin, once said something very profound about color that has always stuck with me. He said that there's no such thing as good colors, only good color relationships. I'm not sure I completely agree (there are some colors that I do appreciate all on their own), but this is a profound point nonetheless. Like notes on a musical scale, colors become beautiful, ugly, intense, or out of place based on the colors that surround them.

FIGURE **4-10** The pink heart surrounded by red

Let's take a pink heart, for example. If we surround the pink heart with red hearts (see Figure 4-10) and more pink hearts, it would look like a card your mom might buy. If we surround that same pink heart with some "edgy" black and gray hearts (see Figure 4-11), it would look like something your kid sister might wear.

The Color Wheel

The color wheel (see Figure 4-12) is a way to view the relationships between all colors. If you plan on doing any kind of art or design with Photoshop, I strongly suggest picking up a physical color wheel. You can usually find one

FIGURE **4-11** The same pink heart surrounded with black and gray

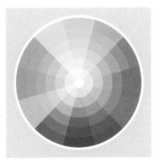

at an art supply store (or even Wal-Mart) for less than $10. That is a sound investment, as you'll shortly see. Although I like to have mine in hand, you can also view color wheels online. Try doing a Google or Wikipedia search for "color wheel."

Looking at a color wheel for the first time, you might be underwhelmed, or possibly even perplexed. It's really a phenomenal way to see the different ways colors work together, as we're about to see.

FIGURE **4-12** A color wheel

Several different color wheels based on different models of color are available. All color wheels have merit, and I'm not going to start a philosophical discussion on which model is better. For our purposes, we'll stick to the RYB (Red, Yellow, Blue) model. This is the color model typically used for painting, and as such, you're more likely to find this color wheel in stores.

Color Relationships

The color wheel is a great way to start looking at the way colors interact. Because the wheel shows color relationships, it becomes an invaluable help in choosing colors to paint or design with. If you get stuck while designing a web site, DVD menu, or digital art piece, you can try one of these color schemes. Let's start by looking at the basics, and then we'll look at more complex ways to combine colors.

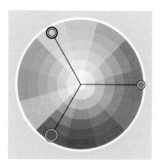

Figure **4-13** The primary colors of the RYB color wheel

Primary Colors Using the RYB color wheel, the three foundational colors are red, yellow, and blue (see Figure 4-13). These are also called the *primary* colors. Knowing that these colors are the base colors helps us as we start looking at other color relationships. We'll look later at using the RGB color model, which is the standard color mode for working in Photoshop.

 Using red, yellow, and blue together when they are bright and fully saturated is a very popular color scheme when designing for an audience of young children.

Secondary Colors When two primary colors are combined, the result is called a *secondary* color (see Figure 4-14). Secondary colors are orange (created by mixing red and yellow), green (yellow + blue), and violet (red + blue).

 When experimenting with color schemes such as primary and secondary colors, you can achieve a similar degree of visual harmony by using desaturated versions of the colors. You can also try using lighter and darker versions of the colors.

Complementary Colors Complementary colors are opposite each other on the color wheel. Complementary colors provide the greatest amount of contrast when used together. Because of that, you'll see these combinations all over the place. Check out Figure 4-15 to see some examples of complementary colors.

Figure **4-15** The LA Lakers and Christmas derive their color schemes from complementary colors.

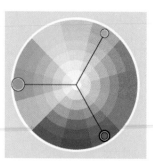

Figure **4-14** The secondary colors of the RYB color wheel

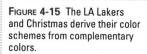

Notice any colors of any famous sports teams or holidays? (See the figure caption for answers to the riddle.)

Note Another familiar set of complementary colors is blue and orange, used often in business web sites.

Because of their high contrast when used together, complementary colors are best used sparingly, especially when fully saturated. Purple and yellow look great on a basketball uniform, but if you were to create yellow text on a purple background, you'd inadvertently create a visual substitute for ipecac. So do the world a favor, and use complementary colors prudently.

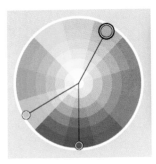

Figure 4-16 A split complementary color scheme

Split Complementary Colors   Split complementary colors are closely related to complementary colors. However, instead of using colors opposite each other on the color wheel, one color is chosen, and then both of the colors on either side of the complement are used. In other words, instead of using the color across the wheel, it uses the colors next door to the color across the wheel. See Figure 4-16 for a diagram of how split complements are determined.

Analogous Colors   The word "analogous" means comparable, or similar. Analogous colors are ones that are right next to each other on the color wheel. For example, looking at the color wheel, we see that violet, blue-violet, and blue are analogous colors. In Figure 4-17, we see an example of these analogous colors in action in a sample design.

Tip Try going to www.google.com, clicking the Images button, and doing a search on a particular color scheme (for example, complementary, analogous, and so on). You'll find many examples of each, showing the color relationships in paintings, home interiors, and more.

Figure 4-17 An analogous color scheme in a design

Color and Media

You can use different color models (or ways of looking at color) depending on the medium (print, web, video, and so on) you're using. This is because color behaves differently when it's being created by different means. For example, if you had a red color and wanted to make it pink, you would *add* white light if you were working with a file to be output to the Internet or a TV screen. If you were trying to do the same thing with a file that would be printed, you would create pink from red by *subtracting* red ink.

Understanding the behavior of color models is absolutely essential to working with color in Photoshop, because this program is used all over the world by professionals in every medium. Many color adjustments work differently depending on the color space used in the current document.

Although Photoshop has a few different color models, we're going to stick to the two most common: RGB and CMYK.

RGB Color

RGB (Red, Green, Blue) is the color model used for describing color with light. If you are a web designer, or if you do video work, or if your final output will always be to a screen or monitor, then you will always want to use the RGB color mode for your documents. This is because colors on monitors and screens are created with light, and red, green, and blue are the components of light.

RGB is often called *additive* color. This is because we add more color in RGB mode to get to white. This makes sense if you think about it. If you had a green spotlight shining on a white wall, the color would be green. If you increase the power of the spotlight, eventually the color would probably become white. It's important to remember that a lot of R and a lot of G and a lot of B make white in RGB mode. Likewise, as with light, the complete removal of R, G, and B will result in black.

CMYK Color

The other big color model that you might deal with often is CMYK, which stands for Cyan, Magenta, Yellow, and blacK. These four colors are the color components of ink and are used for most printed art. Why are these four colors used for ink instead of RGB? That's a subject beyond the scope of this book, but it deals with the control of the reflection of light. Because of this, CMY is the direct opposite of RGB. In the RGB spectrum, cyan and red are complementary (or opposite), as are magenta and green, and yellow and blue. So, where does black come in?

In case you're wondering why black is represented by the letter *K*, it's because K is actually short for "key." *Key* is a printer term for the black used to register and calibrate a printing press. Black is also abbreviated as K to avoid confusion with blue (B).

Because CMYK is the opposite of RGB, CMYK is referred to as *subtractive* color. That means to get to white, we'd have to subtract all colors, as opposed to RGB, where we add colors to get to white. In theory then, we should be able to get to black by adding C, M, and Y together. Or so it would seem. The reality is that because of the limitations of the physical properties of inks, CMY can't quite pull off black. So, we bring in black ink to compensate for CMY's inadequacies.

The number of colors that can be produced with ink (CMYK) is much smaller than the number of colors that can be created with light (RGB). This is one of the biggest reasons why the colors you print do not match what you see on your computer screen.

About Spot Color

It can be a real headache having a great design with amazing colors and not being able to print it correctly. The good news is that there is a solution. The bad news is that it can be a pain to work with, and it costs a fortune. The solution I'm referring to is spot colors. Spot colors are additional inks that can be used in the printing process that aren't mixed with the other inks. The other CMYK inks are often called "process colors" because they create colors by mixing together before printing.

Another benefit of spot colors is that they are spot-on accurate (pun intended). Because they are custom inks that don't mix with the others, they will always look exactly the same no matter where in the world or on what equipment they are printed. For this reason, spot colors are often used for companies like Coca-Cola that have a certain color closely tied to their brand identity.

The most popular spot color company in the United States is called Pantone, which is why spot colors sometimes are called Pantone colors. This is somewhat similar to how a facial tissue is often generically called a Kleenex.

Spot colors are amazing, yes, but you definitely pay the price for the magic. For more information on spot colors, consult Photoshop's Help. When using spot colors, you'll want to maintain close communication with your print provider to make sure there aren't any costly misunderstandings.

Working with Color in Photoshop

Now we'll look at how to apply all that we've been learning about color. In my opinion, Photoshop deals with color very intuitively; it all just makes sense. For the rest of this chapter, we'll be looking at various ways color is used in Photoshop. This will lay a great foundation for the things you will learn in the rest of the book.

The Adobe Color Picker

The Adobe Color Picker is a tool used for choosing colors. These colors can then be used for painting, filling areas with color, and a whole bunch of other things. You'll find this same Color Picker in almost every Adobe application. That's a good thing, too, because it's the most intuitive way I've seen to select colors.

 Your operating system also has a color picker, although the Windows color picker hasn't been updated since Windows 98. You can use the Adobe Color Picker to find a color, and then copy and paste its numbers into your system color picker if that's easier for you.

In Photoshop, the quickest way to access the Color Picker is by clicking once on either of the two swatches at the bottom of the Tools panel.

We've looked briefly at the Adobe Color Picker in previous chapters, but let's take a closer look (see Figure 4-18). On the right side of the Color Picker window, we see a bunch of letters and radio buttons. If you look closely (and read vertically), you'll see our familiar friends RGB and CMYK among the ranks. But what exactly do these buttons do?

Figure 4-18 The Adobe Color Picker

These radio buttons allow you to change which color model you're using to select a color. I find the HSB model the easiest to understand. HSB stands for Hue, Saturation, and Brightness (aka Lightness). This is also the default color model for the Color Picker. You'll notice that the H radio button is selected (see Figure 4-18).

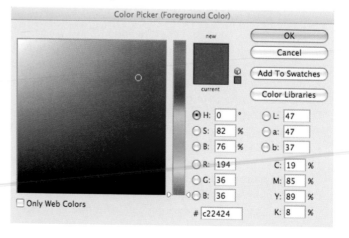

FIGURE 4-19 Click in this bar, or drag the arrows to select a hue.

The radio button that is selected controls what is seen in the narrow bar in the center of the Color Picker. Because H is selected by default, the narrow bar shows us a range of hues to choose from. Because HSB is such an intuitive color model (and is the default), we'll focus on that model for selecting color. After you feel comfortable with the Color Picker, try experimenting with other color models.

Picking the Hue

Now that we know what hue is, what we're doing in this section will make more sense. To select a hue, click anywhere in that skinny, vertical bar in the center of the Color Picker (see Figure 4-19). You can also fine-tune the hue you've selected by dragging vertically on the arrows on the sides of this bar.

Adjusting Saturation and Brightness

Now that we have a hue, it's time to get this color exactly the way we want it by adjusting saturation and brightness. We adjust both attributes in the big square on the left of the Color Picker. To select a color in the big square, just click on the color you want. At first, this square probably just seems like a big mess of colors all thrown together. But these colors are actually arranged in a very intelligent way.

To adjust saturation, adjust the little circle horizontally. Colors on the right are saturated, while colors on the left are desaturated (see Figure 4-18). If you look along the left edge, you'll notice only shades of gray.

Similarly to how we set saturation, we adjust brightness by selecting different colors along the vertical axis. Colors at the top are completely bright, while colors along the bottom are completely dark.

To sum up, we pick colors by starting with the hue (in the center of the Color Picker), and then we fine-tune the saturation and brightness in the bigger square in the Color Picker. The upper-right area shows you your previous color (on the bottom), and your new color (on the top). In that way you can compare and contrast the old and new colors easily (see Figure 4-20).

FIGURE 4-20 The previous color is on the bottom, and the top color swatch shows you the new color that you're picking in the Color Picker.

Testing Your Color Picking Skills

Think you've got this color picking stuff down pat? Try to create these colors in your Color Picker:

How to... Understand the Color Picker Warnings

Not to sound ominous, but you should be aware of a couple of warnings in the Color Picker. You'll find these right next to new/current swatches in the upper-right area of the Color Picker.

The top warning resembles a yellow triangle with an exclamation point in it. This indicates that the currently selected color cannot be reproduced using CMYK inks. So, if you were to print a document using this color, it wouldn't look like that color when it was printed. Technically, we would call this color "out of gamut," or outside of the range of what CMYK is capable of. But thankfully, Photoshop offers you an alternative color right below the warning. If you click that swatch, the CMYK-safe color will be chosen for you.

The other warning, immediately below the CMYK warning, similarly lets you know that the currently selected color is not a web-safe color. As with the CMYK warning, click the swatch below the warning to select the safe color that Photoshop has suggested as an alternative.

Cheating the Color Picker

Instead of dragging around to create colors, you can manually input number values on the right side of the Color Picker. Every number has a color, but the numbers that describe that color change based on the color model used. For example, RGB numbers have three values (one for each of R, G, and B) that range from 0 to 255. So, an RGB color might be 35, 128, 87. CMYK values return four values from 0 to 100%. This refers to how much ink is used to create the color. A percentage of 0 means that the ink is not used for that color, and 100% means that it is used at the maximum amount. A standard CMYK color might be listed as 56, 0, 86, 15.

The field with a number sign at the bottom of the Color Picker is used for hexadecimal colors. Hexadecimal numbers are typically used to describe colors on the Web. A hexadecimal number might look like 8c24cf. I know it looks weird. But you can type those in as well. Or you can reverse the process if you have a web application that is requesting a color from you and you don't know its hexadecimal equivalent. You can use the Adobe Color Picker to find it and generate the hexadecimal number for you. Then just copy and paste the hexadecimal number from the Color Picker into your web application.

If you like a particular color, you can click the Add To Swatches button in the Color Picker to automatically store it in your Swatches panel.

Using Swatches

Figure 4-21 The Swatches panel

Just like at a paint or carpet store, swatches in Photoshop are little samples of color. Swatches are stored in the Swatches panel (see Figure 4-21). If your Swatches panel is not visible, you can go to the Window menu at the top of the interface and select Swatches. All the little squares in the Swatches panel are saved colors that can be used at any time.

If you click one of the swatches in the Swatches panel, it will become your new foreground color in the Tools panel. In the next chapter, we'll talk more in depth about the foreground color and how to use it. You can also save your current foreground color as a swatch by clicking the Create New Swatch Of Foreground Color button.

Photoshop ships with a large collection of swatch libraries, most of them of spot colors. You can load them by going to the Swatches panel fly-out menu and clicking on the name of the swatch library you wish to load.

The Eyedropper Tool

The Eyedropper tool is very helpful for selecting colors you find elsewhere. Let's say, for example, you have a photo of a beautiful sunset, and you want to create some text that is the same color as one of the orange tones in the sunset. You can click that orange color with the Eyedropper tool, and it will become your new foreground color.

FIGURE 4-22 The Eyedropper tool in the Tools panel

To use the Eyedropper tool, open an image, and select the Eyedropper tool from the Tools panel (see Figure 4-22). Then just click anywhere on an image to sample the color from it.

 When you have the Adobe Color Picker open, it turns your cursor into a temporary Eyedropper tool, no matter what tool is selected. So, you can move your cursor outside of the Color Picker and pick a color from an open document if you wish.

5

Getting Creative

How to...

- Paint in Photoshop
- Work with brushes
- Work more efficiently by using painting shortcuts
- Use gradients

The first few chapters have been mostly foundational, setting us up to do great things. Now, with great pleasure, I will introduce you to some fantastic creative tools in Photoshop. Most books and training I've seen on Photoshop deal only with photography and completely ignore the artistic side of this amazing program. Of course, in a book about how to do everything in Photoshop, we'll cover image editing (starting in Chapter 7). But it is now our privilege to investigate the things in Photoshop that inspire, the things that allow us to create from scratch.

We'll look at brushes and Photoshop's powerful painting engine. You'll learn to create *gradients,* which allow us to blend multiple colors together smoothly. You'll also be introduced to a completely different technology: *vector shapes.* Finally, you'll look at a wide array of nondestructive special effects built into Photoshop called *layer styles.* We'll use those layer styles to tremendously enhance the appearance of our paint strokes and vector shapes.

Remember as we go forward that while there are some good rules of thumb for editing images (as we touched on in the previous chapter on color), there are no rules for painting and creating art. I've been fortunate to look over the proverbial shoulder of some of the world's great digital artists, and they do all sorts of stuff "wrong." These tools are fairly straightforward and easy to use. What unlocks their potential is the talent you bring to the table. And even then, Photoshop's tools are here to help out the talentless creative mind. I can't draw a circle to save my life. But I know how to get Photoshop to make one for me. Just let yourself go and be creative. If you've never done that before, then welcome to a new beginning.

Intro to Brushes and Painting

In this section, we're going to look at brushes and painting. You might be curious as to why those are two separate entities. Brushes are objects in Photoshop with limitless ability. You can use them to instantly create fields of grass or an entire document full of multicolored confetti—with one mouse click!

Even more than that, you can use brushes throughout Photoshop. Obviously, you can use brushes to paint and create art, but they are also used by other tools. You use brushes to erase, fix texture problems, and to perform other tasks as well. Even if you only edit photos in Photoshop, this section on painting will be extremely helpful for you.

If you own the Extended version of Photoshop, painting with 3D objects has been vastly expanded in CS4. You can now paint directly on 3D objects to change their diffuse maps. Not only that, but you can also paint directly into other channels as well, such as bump map, reflectivity, self-illumination, and several others. And these 3D features work amazingly well. If you don't have Photoshop CS4 Extended or don't plan on working with 3D files, sorry for the supernerdy tech gibberish. But if you're interested, we'll take a look at Photoshop's Extended features in Chapter 12.

The Repetitious Nature of Brushes

Before we get to playing around with brushes, you need to know what even many experienced Photoshop users don't know: a brush is just a shape. That's it. When you create a paint stroke, you're only duplicating the shape that comprises that paintbrush. Seriously. You may want to reread this paragraph a few times until that sinks in. But even then you may not quite believe me, so let me prove it to you.

First, create a new blank Photoshop document with the default settings. Then create a new blank layer so that we can just throw this layer out once we're done playing with it. Make sure the blank layer is selected in the Layers panel before moving on. Next, select the Brush tool in the Tools panel.

 You can also select the Brush tool by using the easy-to-remember keyboard shortcut, "B." That's it! Just press B on your keyboard, and the Brush tool will be selected.

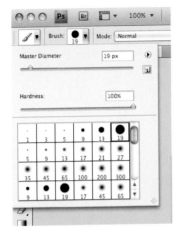

Then, in the Options bar (at the top of the interface), click the Brush Preset picker, as shown in Figure 5-1.

At the bottom of this drop-down, you can see a collection of premade brushes for you to choose from. The number at the bottom indicates how large the brush is. I'm going to select the Hard Round 19 px (pixels) brush from the upper-right corner.

Now you're ready to paint. However, you need to choose a color to paint with. When you paint, the color of the paint is the foreground color, which is the upper-left color swatch at the bottom of the Tools panel (white, as shown here). Click the foreground color swatch to open the Color Picker, select a color, and click OK.

FIGURE 5-1 The Brush Preset picker in the Options bar

Note For most tasks involving color, you will use the foreground color. The other swatch, the background color, is not used nearly as often.

In the top area of the new document, drag with your mouse to create a paint stroke. It should look like an ordinary paint stroke (see Figure 5-2).

But now let's open up the hood of this paintbrush and see what's going on. For that, we'll need to open the Brushes panel. If the Brushes panel is not currently showing in your interface, just click the Window menu at the top of the interface and select Brushes.

FIGURE 5-2 The result of painting with the Hard Round 19 px brush

You can also start your paint stroke outside of the document. This is especially useful for creating paint along document edges, such as for frames.

The Brushes panel, shown in Figure 5-3, is the headquarters of the Photoshop painting engine. Although you can access basic brush options from many places in Photoshop, this is the only place you can find the most powerful of the brush options available to you. At first glance, this panel may intimidate. But here's how it works—the list on the left side of the panel is where we choose the category of options we want to adjust. The big square area on the right is where we make those adjustments.

Photoshop often likes to organize large amounts of data the way it does in the Brushes panel. You'll see this same layout in the preferences, layer styles, and more. In all of these places, you click on the left to select a category and then click on the right to adjust the parameters of that category.

On the left side of the Brushes panel, select the category Brush Tip Shape. The right side of the panel updates to show you options for the brush tip shape (see Figure 5-4).

FIGURE 5-3 The Brushes panel

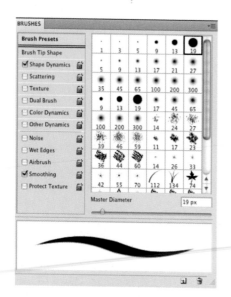

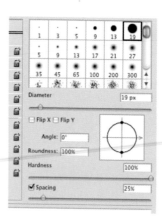

FIGURE 5-4 The options in the Brush Tip Shape area

FIGURE 5-5 The result of painting with the same paintbrush after increasing the spacing

At the bottom of this panel is a property called Spacing. This determines how far apart the brush repeats the original shape when you paint with this brush. Drag this option to the right to increase the space between the circle shapes that this brush is made of. After increasing the Spacing parameter a bit (to 120% or so), you can see that this brush is simply a circle duplicated many times. Now try painting in your document again below your original paint stroke, and check out the magic (see Figure 5-5). Try doing *that* with a real paintbrush!

Sometimes it pays to reduce the spacing. When creating a large paint stroke (or a regular-sized paint stroke in a lower-resolution document such as a web graphic), you may notice that the paint stroke is not completely smooth. See Figure 5-6 for a typical instance of this. What's happening is that the paint strokes are so big that they are not close enough when painted, and you're seeing the gaps between the repetitions of the shape. To fix this, simply reduce the Spacing value to bring the repetitions closer together.

Adjusting Basic Brush Properties

Now that we understand what's going on behind the scenes with brushes, let's back up a bit and look at some of the more basic properties of brushes.

FIGURE 5-6 When the brush size is large, sometimes spaces can be seen between shape repetitions.

About Brush Size

Perhaps the most important brush property is size. It's the one I find myself fiddling with most often. Thankfully, your mouse cursor actually turns into a shape that represents the size (and shape) of your paintbrush when the Brush tool is selected.

Note If you don't see a cursor shaped like your paintbrush, go to the Cursors area of the preferences to make sure you have the correct painting cursor settings. If that doesn't work, make sure that CAPS LOCK is off.

That brings me to some of the most useful keyboard shortcuts—the brush size shortcuts. You can adjust brush size in a variety of ways (such as using the Brushes panel), but the best way is to use the bracket keys on your keyboard. They look like this: [and]. Pressing the [key on your keyboard will decrease the size of your brush, while pressing the] key will increase it.

How to... Adjust Brushes

You have several ways to adjust basic brush parameters such as size, shape, and hardness. One of the ways we've looked at uses the Brushes panel. The Brushes panel is certainly the most powerful way to do it, but it's probably also the most inconvenient.

As I mentioned at the beginning of this chapter, you can also use the Options bar at the top of the interface to adjust basic brush properties. Most of these options are stored in the Brush Preset picker we looked at earlier. Remember that the Options bar is context sensitive, so you won't see brush options here unless you have a tool, like the Brush tool, that actually uses brushes.

Perhaps the quickest and easiest way to adjust basic brush properties is by right-clicking while using a tool that uses brushes. The right-click menu that appears closely resembles the Brush Preset picker drop-down found in the Options bar.

I'm partial to the right-clicking method, as it's the least disturbing to the creative process. But Photoshop provides multiple ways to do the same thing for a reason; no one way is more or less correct than another. It's all about your preference—except when it comes to the keyboard shortcuts, [and]. Using those not only allows you to change the size more easily than by using any menu, but with the keyboard shortcuts, you can also dynamically see the size of the brush as you increase it. You can't do that with adjustments made from the menus.

This is really helpful because sometimes you find the perfect brush shape and behavior, but it's way too big or too small. Knowing how to adjust brush size solves your problem. You can make any brush significantly smaller or larger than it is.

 Brushes are based on shapes made with pixels. Custom brushes that are resized and enlarged too much may create paint strokes that appear pixelated.

About Brush Hardness

Brush hardness refers to the edge of the shape used to create the brush. See Figure 5-7 for the difference between a hard-edged brush and a soft-edged brush. Edges that are soft are essentially feathered, or in other words, blurry. Feathered edges are good for blending colors together.

To adjust hardness, you can go to either the Brushes panel or the Options bar, or you can right-click in the document with the Brush tool selected. Remember that increasing hardness reduces

FIGURE 5-7 A hard-edged brush (top) and a soft-edged brush (bottom)

the blur on the edge. If you're wondering if there's another amazing shortcut for adjusting brush hardness, there is. Just hold down SHIFT while you're using the bracket shortcuts ([and]). Using SHIFT-[will decrease the hardness (thereby increasing softness), and using SHIFT-] will increase the hardness.

Tip   Wondering how I create such straight lines when I've already confessed to extremely poor drawing skills? Simply click once, and then hold SHIFT and click another spot. Photoshop will automatically create a straight line from the first point to the next.

About Brush Shape

Since brushstrokes are just repeated shapes, what if we used more than just circles to paint? The answer is that we'd make some really cool stuff. Let's play around a little.

Note   If you want to start with a fresh canvas (which I recommend), then you can undo the paint strokes; otherwise, delete the layer you painted on, and create a new one for this exercise.

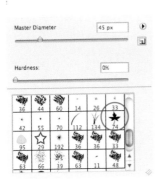

FIGURE 5-8 The Scattered Maple Leaves brush, shown here in the right-click menu

Open a collection of brush shapes by going to any of the places we've used to adjust other brush properties. Scroll down to select the Scattered Maple Leaves brush. See Figure 5-8 if you're having difficulty locating it.

This brush is special, unlike anything we've looked at so far. To let this brush do its thing, you need to select a good color before painting. Click the foreground color in the Tools panel to open the Color Picker and select an orange color. If you'd like to use the RGB numbers for the orange I selected, they are 188, 127, 39. Next, drag only once in your document, and look at that—holy autumn, Batman! (see Figure 5-9).

How is it possible to drag once and create all of this autumn madness? You made multiple leaves, but they were also scattered randomly, and they were given a variety of colors as well. The answer lies in Photoshop's ability to customize brushes. In the Brushes panel, you can scatter brushes and create random color. Sometimes paintbrushes are more than they appear to be. In Chapter 14, we'll look at many of these options, as well as how to load new brush libraries into Photoshop (which ships with several collections of brushes) and where to find free brushes on the Web.

FIGURE 5-9 Painting with the Scattered Maple Leaves brush and an orange color

Did You Know?

How to Paint with a Mouse

No matter how much talent you have (or don't have) painting in the real world, trying to paint in Photoshop with a mouse can be maddening. Can you imagine trying to paint with a laptop?

There is a solution. It's called a *graphics tablet,* also called a stylus pen or a graphic pen. Basically, it's a little tablet that you connect to your computer (usually via USB), and it comes with a pen. The pen functions like a mouse on the tablet. So, if you draw a happy face on the tablet with the pen, it will paint a happy face in Photoshop.

Not only does this tablet recognize the pen for input, but most tablets (even the cheap ones) also recognize the pressure you apply while painting. I have an old tablet that was $79 that has 512 levels of sensitivity. Newer or more expensive models have even more sensitivity. Other models also recognize more from the pen, such as how much it is tilted or rotated, which is really helpful for digital calligraphy.

But this story gets even better. Photoshop is specifically built to respond to these tablets. You can tell Photoshop that when you press harder, it should automatically make the brush size larger. Or you can set it so that as you press more lightly with the pen, it makes the paint more transparent or scatters it less or changes colors—or all of the above. You can also adjust other parameters with the tablet.

To get Photoshop to recognize and use a tablet, go to the Brushes panel and find a property that has a Control drop-down list. From the drop-down list, select Pen Pressure to control that property by using the pen and graphics tablet. Graphics tablets really help you get the most out of the paint capabilities of Photoshop. The most common manufacturer of graphics tablets is Wacom (pronounced WALK-em), and their tablets can be found online and in many stores that sell computers and peripherals.

Some brushes, such as this Scattered Maple Leaves brush, will not allow you to adjust certain properties such as hardness.

As powerful at painting as Photoshop is, the most powerful painting program is Corel Painter. Painter even allows you to change the type of bristles on brushes and to change colors of individual bristles as you can in the real world.

More Invaluable Painting Shortcuts

I just can't live without a couple of other painting shortcuts. The first one goes back to something that we covered in Chapter 2. Remember that you can hold the SPACEBAR to temporarily toggle the Hand tool, which allows you to pan around a document. This is extremely useful while you're painting. Many times when painting, you'll be zoomed in closely, and the enlarged document won't fit in the work area. Because of this closeness, you'll want to pan around a lot. You can imagine how time-consuming it would be (and how it would interrupt the creative flow) to keep going back and forth to the Tools panel to switch tools. Don't do that. Just hold down the SPACEBAR to change the cursor into the Hand tool, drag to move the document, and then release the SPACEBAR to get the Brush tool back and to continue painting.

Another great painting tip deals with sampling colors while painting. Let's say you have an image like the one in Figure 5-10.

FIGURE 5-10 The castle image

The image shown in Figure 5-10 was created by a talented illustrator and good friend, Will Kindrick. It doesn't really have much to do with what we're doing here, but in case you're curious, this art was created in another Adobe application called Adobe Illustrator. We'll talk briefly about what Illustrator does later in this chapter.

Suppose you want to print this image on a poster that is larger than the image. If we just stretch the image to fit the poster, it won't look so great. But what we could do without losing any image quality is to expand the canvas of this document, which would create more blank space around the document. We can then expand the background pixels of this image by using painting tools.

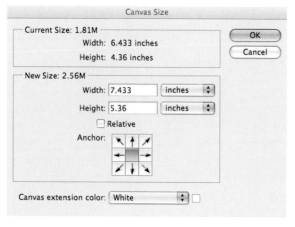

FIGURE 5-11 The Canvas Size dialog box with the new size

Go to the Image menu and select Canvas Size. That opens the Canvas Size dialog box (see Figure 5-11). We probably want to increase this document by about a half inch in all directions. To do that, we'll need to increase the width and height by 1 inch each. So, change the Width value to **7.433** inches, and the Height value **to 5.36** inches. Make sure that the Canvas extension color is set to White, and click OK.

This expands the size of the document by a half inch on all sides. Now, we can paint more of the background to expand the landscape around the castle.

After trying to paint for a minute, you'll probably run into a frustrating problem. There are a few different colors here. It's a real pain to go and select the Eyedropper tool in the Tools panel every time you want to paint a different part of the image. The great secret is to hold down the ALT (Windows)/OPT (Mac) key while you are using the Brush tool. This will temporarily toggle the Eyedropper tool. You can sample a color, paint with it, and then hold ALT/OPT to sample more colors and keep painting. This trick works especially well with really defined colors like the ones in this image. If this were a photograph, shadows and soft edges all over the place would make it more challenging.

Make sure that every time you paint, it's on a new, blank layer. When painting more than a few strokes, you should create a new layer and start painting on that.

Using Gradients

FIGURE **5-12** A gradient created with the Gradient tool. Note that the blend is smooth.

Gradients are the smooth blending of two or more colors. They're used widely in Photoshop. To learn about them, we're going to stick to using the Gradient tool in the Tools panel. Once you get comfortable with using this tool, you'll be able to use gradients skillfully throughout Photoshop.

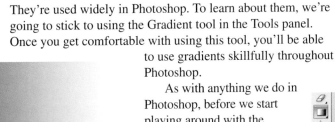

As with anything we do in Photoshop, before we start playing around with the Gradient tool, create a new blank layer to create gradients on. Next, select the Gradient tool in the Tools panel.

To use the Gradient tool, make sure that the new blank layer is selected, and then drag in your document from one side of the document to the other. Your colors might be different than mine (which is okay for now), but essentially one color was created where you first clicked, and another color was created where you let go of the mouse, and everything in between was a smooth blended transition between the two (see Figure 5-12).

Before we change the color, be aware that where you drag your mouse controls how these colors blend together. Draw the gradient again (which you can do on top of the existing gradient—it will in effect paint over the original gradient), but this time instead of clicking from one end of the document to another, click in the middle of the document. Then move your cursor a little, and let go of the mouse button. The result is very different because you've told Photoshop that the transition between colors should now be much shorter (see Figure 5-13).

FIGURE **5-13** The result of a shorter drag with the Gradient tool

Note You don't have to drag the Gradient tool only from side to side. You can drag in any direction to create a gradient. You can also begin to draw (or end) the gradient outside the image if you want to leave one of the colors out of the document.

Changing Gradient Colors

Changing the colors of gradients is a little tricky, both to access and to adjust. To do this, go to the Options bar with the Gradient tool selected. This next part is where it's easy to click the wrong thing. In the Options bar is a thumbnail preview of your gradient, with a little drop-down arrow to its right. See Figure 5-14 for a close-up. The trick with this is that it's actually two buttons—the gradient and the arrow—and clicking the gradient will produce a different result than clicking the arrow.

FIGURE 5-14 The gradient drop-down in the Options bar is actually two buttons.

Click the arrow to choose from a set of gradients that ship with Photoshop. Click the gradient itself to access the Gradient Editor, shown in Figure 5-15, and manually change the colors of your gradient.

 Note You can also choose from the gradient presets in the Gradient Editor.

At the bottom of the Gradient Editor, you'll see your gradient with little icons (they look like tiny houses to me) both above and below every color. These are called *color stops*. Right now, we're only going to be concerned with the bottom stops. Double-click one of these to open the Color Picker, and choose a new color for that area of the gradient. You can also click in a blank area at the bottom of the gradient to add multiple colors to the gradient. Or you can drag gradient color stops closer together to adjust the transition between colors. Once you're done editing, click OK to accept your gradient; then drag with the Gradient tool to make sweet gradient goodness.

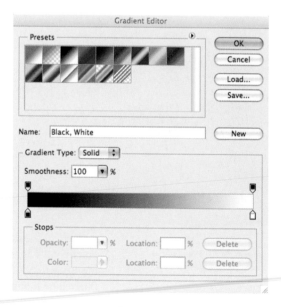

FIGURE 5-15 The Gradient Editor

Tip   The top stop controls the opacity of that area of the gradient. Use this to control the transparency of certain areas of your gradient.

Changing the Type of Gradient

FIGURE 5-16 A radial gradient

You can also change the shape of the gradient by clicking the buttons in the Options bar when the Gradient tool is selected. If you are like 99 percent of Photoshop users, you will probably only ever use linear gradients (the first button) and radial gradients (the second button).

The term *linear* means relating to a line. Linear gradients are the ones that we've looked at so far that just create gradations in one direction.

Radial gradients (see Figure 5-16) create gradients that start from a center point and radiate out from around that point. Radial gradients are great for creating focus in the center of a design or for creating sunbursts.

Using Gradients

Gradients are useful in art as well as design. Notice what a gradient adds to the background of the design shown in Figure 5-17. Note also that the effect is very subtle, but it does make a big difference. Subtly using gradients in backgrounds and other elements of design is very popular right now in print, on the Web, and in video.

FIGURE 5-17 Notice the difference that a gradient makes in the background of this design.

Gradients are also often used for special effects, especially to create metallic looks. Figure 5-18 shows a gradient preset that ships with Photoshop that attempts to re-create a metallic look by using only a gradient. Notice the multiple colors in this gradient, as well as the fact that the stops have been adjusted to be closer to each other to create more abrupt transitions between some of the colors.

FIGURE 5-18 A metallic gradient that ships with Photoshop. It kind of looks like a tube.

Intro to Vectors and Shapes

We're now going to venture into foreign territory to talk about vector shapes. So far, everything we've looked at has been created by pixels. Sometimes art is not built with pixels, but is built instead with mathematical equations called *vectors*. Vector graphics are a little more complex, as you might imagine. They are created with anchor points, segments, tangents, and handles.

The great benefit of vector shapes is that because they are made with math, they are infinitely scalable. You can increase and decrease their size indefinitely, and you can take an object that was created very small and blow it up to fit on a billboard without losing any quality in either instance. That's not the case with art created with pixels. Figure 5-19 shows two circles: one raster (that is, made with pixels) and one vector. Figure 5-20 shows those same circles enlarged. It will be immediately apparent how useful vector shapes are.

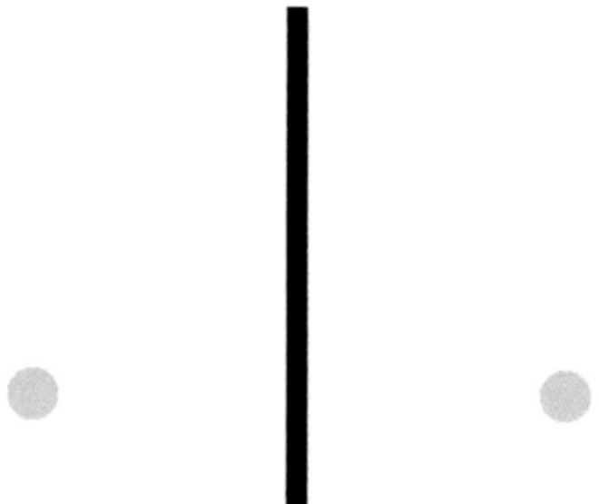

Often when I'm teaching classes about this, someone asks, "Why isn't all art made with vectors?" Because it is very difficult to make vector art look lifelike and organic. Vector art, by its very nature, is more suited to cartoony art, art with flat areas of color. Because of its scalable nature, vector art is also the most common method of creating logos.

FIGURE 5-19 The shape created with pixels is on the left; the one created with vectors is on the right. At this size, they appear identical.

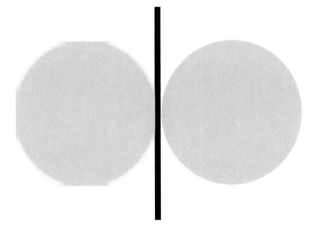

The lion's share of vector art is created in Adobe Illustrator, mentioned earlier in this chapter. The castle image that we looked at is a perfect example of vector art. Everything has a hard edge, and there are big areas of flat color.

Even though Illustrator is the champion of vector art, Photoshop also has some vector capabilities. They aren't nearly as powerful as they are in Illustrator, but they might be more than you would expect out of a pixel-based image editing program.

FIGURE 5-20 Once the shapes are enlarged, the difference between the two is unmistakable.

Creating Shapes

Delving into the ins and outs of vector art creation is beyond the scope of this book. However, we can quickly and easily create vector shapes in Photoshop by using one of the many shapes that ship with the program. The vector-based shape tools are found toward the bottom of the Tools panel. Click and hold down your mouse on the Rectangle tool to see all of the shape tools.

To start our journey into the vector realms, we're going to select another tool in this tool slot, the Custom Shape tool. It looks like an amoeba, or maybe like the silhouette of Patrick Star from *SpongeBob*. The other shape tools are just what they say: the Rectangle tool basically creates rectangles, and so forth. But the Custom Shape tool is like a doorway to a whole world of additional vector shapes.

FIGURE 5-21 The shapes in the Shape drop-down in the Options bar

Once you select the Custom Shape tool in the Tools panel, you will see some additional options in the Options bar. The most important new option is the Shape drop-down list. Click that to see the default shapes library, shown in Figure 5-21. As you're drooling in anticipation, keep in mind that these shapes are all completely vector. If you needed to, you could print them the size of Texas (assuming, of course, that you had a Texas-sized printer), and the quality would be perfect. From the Shape drop-down, you'll see many common and helpful shapes such as arrows, a heart, a checkmark, a talk bubble, a copyright mark, and much more.

I'm going to channel my inner Harry Potter and select the lightning bolt shape. Before you create the shape, you'll want to check a few things in the Options bar. First, check the color swatch on the right side of the options to make sure this is the color you want. If you don't approve, click that swatch to open the Color Picker and change it. Next, look on the left side of the Options bar at the group of three icons. It's important that the far left icon is selected (see Figure 5-22). With this icon selected, you don't have to create a new layer for this shape. It will automatically create a layer for you, called a *shape layer*.

FIGURE 5-22 Make sure this button is chosen before creating your shape.

Shape layers are essentially areas of solid color that are masked by a vector shape. Both the fill color and the vector shape remain completely editable.

To create the shape, drag in the main document window. You might notice how easy it is to create a really terrible lightning bolt. To make sure that your horizontal and vertical dimensions remain in proper proportion to each other, hold down SHIFT while creating your shape. When you release your mouse button, you'll have a shape in the document window and a shape layer in the Layers panel (see Figure 5-23). Huzzah!

Modifying Shapes

As we've been playing with shapes, you might have noticed a bunch of dots all around the edges of these shapes. These dots are called *anchor points*. These points can be easily adjusted to change the shape of vector layers. This is another reason why vector shapes are often used for computer drawing.

FIGURE 5-23 After creating the shape layer

You have a few different ways to adjust vector layers. In the tool slot immediately above the spot where we found the Custom Shape tool in the Tools panel are a couple of helpful vector-adjustment tools. They are two arrows, one black and one white. The black arrow is called the Path Selection tool, and its primary purpose is to select and move entire paths. "Paths" is another name for vector shapes.

If you want to adjust individual anchor points or the segments that connect them, use the white arrow—the Direct Selection tool. With the Direct Selection tool selected, drag one of the points to move it (see Figure 5-24). You can also drag segments to move those around.

In Chapter 10, we'll look at how to transform objects, or in other words, scale, rotate, and so forth. With objects created with pixels, we'll see how their quality gets reduced with every transformation. However, with shapes, you can

FIGURE 5-24 The lightning bolt shape after moving an anchor point

transform and manipulate them as much and as often as you'd like, with absolutely no reduction in quality.

Using Layer Styles

Layer styles are special effects you can apply to layers. These special effects include such things as shadows, glow effects, pseudo 3D effects, strokes around objects, and more. My favorite aspect of these effects is that they can be adjusted or removed at any time. Even after you save the document and close Photoshop, the layer styles will be completely editable when you reopen the document. Now, we'll look at how to apply layer styles. In Chapter 14, we'll revisit layer styles, and look at them a little more in depth.

FIGURE 5-25 You can double-click the blank area next to the layer name to open the Layer Style dialog box.

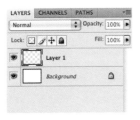

Applying Layer Styles

To apply layer styles, you can click on the fx icon at the bottom of the Layers panel. But to use this method, you'll want to know ahead of time which effect you want to apply. Alternatively, you could use my favorite way to apply layer styles: just double-click a layer in the blank area to the right of its name (see Figure 5-25).

You cannot apply layer styles to a background layer.

If you opened the Layer Style dialog box, go ahead and click Cancel to close it. Before we actually apply anything, we need to create something to apply a style to. If we apply, say, an Outer Glow effect to a blank layer, or even to a full-size layer that is filled with color, we won't see the glow (because it creates a glow on the outside of the layer). Layer styles work best with shapes, text, and other objects that are smaller than the document.

FIGURE 5-26 The paint stroke

In this case, we'll apply styles to a paint stroke. I'll select the Brush tool in the Tools panel, and then select the Hard Round 19 px brush we used at the beginning of this chapter. And, as at the beginning of this chapter, we'll go to the Brushes panel and increase the Spacing value. Make sure that your foreground color is not black or white. Then paint a paint stroke with this brush on a new layer (see Figure 5-26).

Next, double-click the layer to the right of its name to open the Layer Style dialog box. As with the Brushes panel, the effects on the left are like categories. Click the check box to turn effects on or off. Click the name of the effect to see the options for that effect in the big area on the right side of the dialog box.

Let's start by applying the most common of layer style effects, Drop Shadow. In the Layer Style dialog box, make sure that the Preview check box on the far right is checked. This will allow you to preview the result of your changes as you make them. Click Drop Shadow on the left side of the Layer Style dialog box. This instantly adds a drop shadow behind the paint stroke (see Figure 5-27).

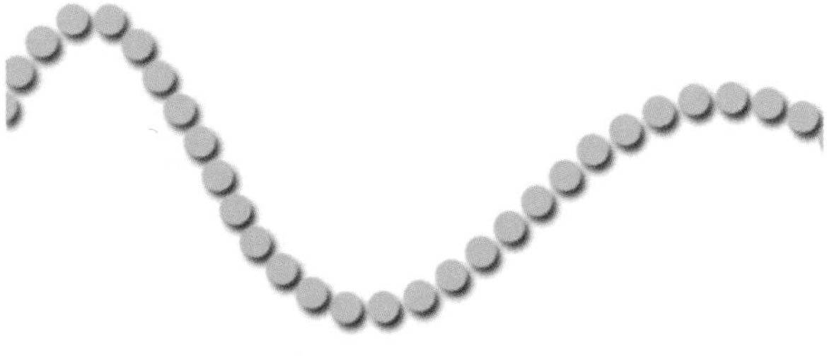

FIGURE 5-27 The paint stroke with a drop shadow applied

Drop shadows are used to make objects appear distinct from their background. *Compositing,* or combining multiple elements into the same scene, is also greatly assisted by drop shadows. Drop shadows are also used to create a kind of 3D effect. With the drop shadow applied, you'll notice how the paint stroke now appears to float in front of the background. You can customize the shadow by adjusting the parameters on the right.

Next, let's add an Outer Glow to this paint stroke. Typically, I wouldn't add both a drop shadow and a glow to the same object; it's just too gaudy in most cases. But we're going to do it here to show you how easy it is to apply multiple effects. Just click Outer Glow. As before, the effect is applied, and the right side of the dialog box changes to show you Outer Glow's options. As you look in your document window, you'll see both the shadow and the glow on your paint stroke. Now, even for demonstration purposes, this looks too terrible to continue. So, click the check mark next to Outer Glow on the left side of the dialog box. This will remove that effect.

FIGURE 5-28 The paint stroke with both a Drop Shadow effect and a Bevel And Emboss effect applied

Finally, let's add another popular effect, Bevel And Emboss. This effect will essentially add a highlight on one side of your object and a shadow on the other. This creates the illusion that your object is 3D. It's a great effect to use in conjunction with a drop shadow to create a 3D look. As before, just click Bevel And Emboss on the left of the Layer Style dialog box to turn it on. Click OK to accept it, and you'll see the final result (see Figure 5-28).

Drop Shadow and Bevel And Emboss are *effects*. A *style* is a collection of effects.

Adjusting Layer Styles

After clicking OK to accept your layer style, you'll notice that the layer with your paint stroke looks a little different.

The fx icon that is now on the right side of your layer serves as a reminder that layer styles have been applied to that layer. Also, on the rightmost edge of the layer is a small drop-down arrow. If you aren't seeing the individual effects in the Layers panel, you can click this arrow to see them. With this open, you can see all layer style effects applied to this layer.

A visibility icon—which looks like an eye—is next to each effect, and next to the word "Effects." Just as with layers, clicking the visibility icon will temporarily hide an effect. Click the visibility icon next to the Bevel And Emboss effect to hide it. Click the same spot again to make it visible again. If you click the visibility icon next to the word "Effects," you'll hide all applied effects at once.

If you like the effects that you've applied, but you just want to change the settings, or if you want to add effects to or remove effects from the layer, just double-click either the name of the effect or the right half of the layer to reopen the Layer Style dialog box. You'll see all your settings there exactly as you left them; make your changes and click OK to update the style.

Creative Mini-Project

Now that we've learned a little about being creative, let's put all of this together in a project. We're going to make a lightning bolt striking, and creating a ball of sparks. Of course, this wouldn't really be a true creative project if I told you to follow all of my instructions to the letter. Feel free to venture off on your own. No matter how great the tutorial or book is, you'll never be good at these creative tools until you explore their potential on your own.

First step, start from scratch. Let's make a new Photoshop document with the default settings. Next, create a new blank layer. We're going to fill this entire layer with black. The fastest way to do this is to press D on your keyboard. This resets the foreground and background colors to their defaults, which are black as foreground and white as background. Next, making sure that the new blank layer is selected in the Layers panel, press the keyboard shortcut ALT-BACKSPACE (Windows)/OPT-DELETE (Mac). This will fill the layer with the foreground color, which is black.

Next, select the Brush tool in the Tools panel. In one of the three ways we discussed earlier in this chapter, select the brush called Fuzzball, which is 192 pixels large, and is on the right side. Then press X on your keyboard, which will eXchange the foreground and background colors. This will make white the foreground color, which is what we want for painting with. Create yet another new layer, this time for the fuzzball painting we'll be doing.

Click one time to paint a single fuzzball at the bottom of the document in the center. Check Figure 5-29 to see what I have so far.

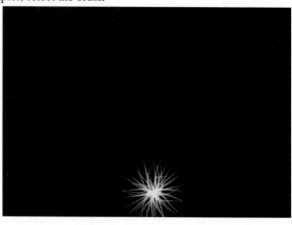

FIGURE 5-29 The project with a black background and a white fuzzball

Tip To get the most out of Photoshop, you'll need to be creative, using objects for purposes other than what they were intended. In this case, we're using a fuzzball as our spark; it totally works!

This project is starting to have a few layers now, so let's name them before going any further. Double-click the name of the black background layer to rename it something more descriptive, like **Black Background**. Do the same thing with the fuzzball layer, renaming it **Sparks** or something similar.

Now, let's add a glow to the spark. Double-click the Sparks layer to the right of its name to open the Layer Style dialog box. Then click Outer Glow on the left side to add a glow. We'll leave the settings at their defaults and click OK. Notice how the glow effect is subtle, but it makes the sparks seem more electric and intense (see Figure 5-30).

FIGURE 5-30 The Sparks layer with an Outer Glow effect applied

This is another of the many reasons to utilize layers in your work. If the fuzzball were on the same layer as the black background, we could not add a glow to it, because the glow would go around the border of the black layer.

Next, let's add the lightning bolt. In the Tools panel, choose the Custom Shape tool. Then, from the Shape drop-down in the Options bar, choose the lightning shape. I'm going to make my lightning black because I'm going to use a layer style that works best with dark colors. As before, drag to create a lightning bolt. If the lightning bolt doesn't end up where you want it, remember that you can always use the Path Selection tool in the Tools panel to move it into place.

 If your lightning bolt appears to have a jagged gray line around it, just click once on the thumbnail of the shape on the shape layer in the Layers panel to deactivate it.

Let's add some effects to this lightning bolt. As with the Sparks layer, let's add an Outer Glow effect here. That creates a glow on the outside of the object. The result so far is pretty cool. But let's also add an Inner Glow effect. This creates a glow on the inside of objects. This time, we're going to adjust some options. After clicking on Inner Glow on the left, you should see its options on the right side of the Layer Style dialog box (see Figure 5-31). In the Elements area in the middle, make

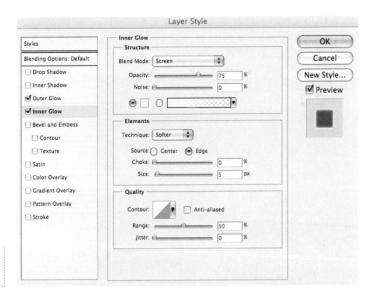

FIGURE 5-31 The Inner Glow options

FIGURE 5-32 After adding inner and outer glows to the lightning bolt

sure that the Choke value is 0% and that the Size value is about 15 px. This will create a larger glow inside the lightning, as shown in Figure 5-32.

If you wanted to change this further, you could click the color swatch at the top of the Inner Glow options. You could also try adding other effects to the lightning bolt, such as Bevel And Emboss. Since we're not going for realism here, just have fun and experiment.

One last adjustment we'll make deals with layer order. Because we created the Sparks layer first, it shows up behind the lightning bolt. That's not how things work! Our sparks need to be in front of the lightning bolt. So, in the Layers panel, drag the Sparks layer on top of the shape layer that contains the lightning bolt. After I fiddled around a bit, my final result can be seen in Figure 5-33.

FIGURE 5-33 My final project

6

Picking Pixels with Selections

How to...

- Use selections
- Select pixels manually with tools
- Select pixels by color
- Refine selection edges

Selections are a critical part of using Photoshop effectively. Selections tell Photoshop which part of the image you want to be affected by edits that you make. Basic selections are extremely easy to make. We'll also look at how to refine selections to get all the pixels we want, and none that we don't.

The Power of Selections

Let's get introduced to selections by seeing them in action. I'm going to open the *sea of daffodils .tif* image. Of course, you should open whatever image you have handy if you'd like to follow along. We'll now apply a filter to this image. Filters are like special effects. In Chapter 13, we'll look more closely at filters. For now, we'll have to settle for a glance.

With your image open, go to the Filter menu at the top of the interface. From the Filter menu, choose Pixelate | Mosaic, to open the Mosaic filter dialog box, shown in Figure 6-1.

In the Mosaic filter dialog box, change the Cell Size value to **60**. This will increase the size of the squares used to make a mosaic out of the image of the daffodils. Then click OK. Notice how the entire image is converted into a mosaic, or large squares each of a single color (see Figure 6-2). Now we'll do the same thing, but we're going to make a selection first to see the difference.

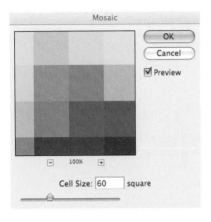

FIGURE 6-1 The Mosaic filter
dialog box

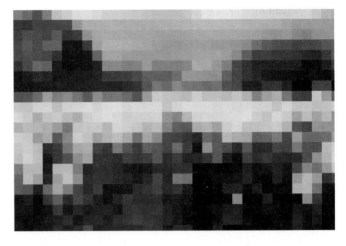

FIGURE 6-2 The *sea of daffodils*
.tif image after applying the Mosaic
effect First, undo the mosaic effect.
Then go to the Tools panel, and
select the Rectangular Marquee
tool, found in the tool slot second
from the top.

Creating selections with the Rectangular Marquee tool is probably the fastest way to create a selection. All you have to do is drag in the document to create a selection area. I'm going to drag in the left side of the document to create a square. Once you release your mouse button, you'll see a rectangle that looks like it has a moving trail of dashes around it (see Figure 6-3). This is why it's called a *marquee*, named after the type of sign over old movie theaters, Vegas casinos, and so on. In nerdy Photoshop circles, we would call these little selection indicators "marching ants," because they look like little ants walking around your selection.

FIGURE 6-3 This rectangular
area indicates that the area is now
selected.

When you're creating rectangular selection areas with the Rectangular Marquee tool, the point where you first click becomes the upper-left corner of the rectangle.

What this little marquee selection tells Photoshop is significant. Basically, it tells Photoshop that only what is in that area is available for editing; everything else in the document is off limits. If you were to select the Brush tool and try to paint outside of that selection rectangle, you'd get really frustrated. That's what selections do—they limit the pixels that Photoshop is allowed to edit.

Now, when we apply the Mosaic filter with this selection active, only what is within the selection area will be affected. To test this, simply go to the Filter menu and select Mosaic (from the top of the Filter menu). The Filter menu stores the last filter that you used, along with all of the settings you changed, at the top of this menu for quick reapplication. After applying the filter, we'll see that only the area within the selection area is affected, as shown in Figure 6-4.

So, what could we use selections for in the real world? We've already seen that they can be set up to limit painting. If you want to paint a certain portion of your image and you don't want to color outside the proverbial lines, you can use selections to keep the paint where you want it. Once a piece of an image is selected, you can also move it or remove it. And, as you'll see, you can have many more reasons for creating and using selections.

FIGURE 6-4 After applying the Mosaic effect to the selected area

The Selection Tools

Now that we know what selections do, let's dig into the tools available for the job. Some tools are easier to use than others, and some are definitely more powerful than others. But never forget that all tools have their place. Even the Rectangular Marquee tool with all of its Neanderthal simplicity is often the tool of choice for selecting boxes, stairs, windows, and other rectangular objects.

The Marquee Tools

Let's look a little more closely at the marquee selection tools, which consist of the Rectangular and the Elliptical Marquee tools. They are simple, but come in handy often. The usefulness of both tools is also greatly enhanced by the use of keyboard shortcuts.

FIGURE 6-5 Holding down SHIFT while creating selections allows you to add to the selection area.

The Rectangular Marquee Tool

We'll start with our now-familiar friend, the Rectangular Marquee tool. We know that we can drag to create a selection area, but there's so much more to the story.

What happens when you have a selection area and you want to create a second selection area? Try doing it. The default behavior is that all selection areas are completely deselected and the new selection appears. But what if you want to have multiple rectangular areas selected at once? The trick is to hold down SHIFT while clicking to create an additional selection, as shown in Figure 6-5.

What happens when you want to remove one of these selection areas, or even part of one of them? The trick is to hold the ALT (Windows)/OPT (Mac) key down while making the selection. Holding this key down will, in effect, turn a selection tool into a kind of selection-eraser tool. This is how you can make a selection that looks like a donut or the state of Utah (see Figure 6-6).

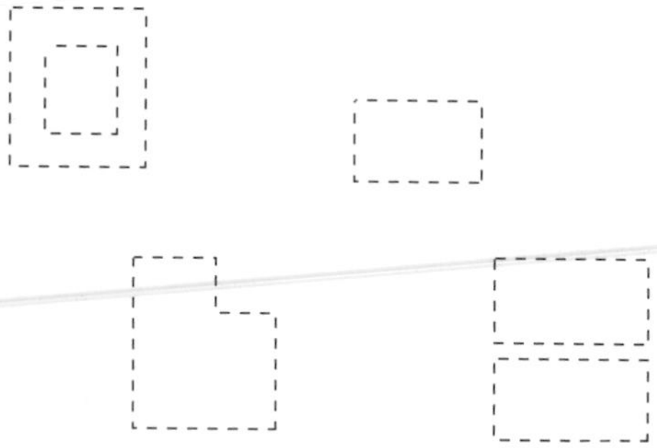

FIGURE 6-6 Holding down the ALT (Windows)/OPT (Mac) key while creating selections allows you to subtract from the selection area.

To deselect a selection area, you can use the keyboard shortcut, CTRL (Windows)/CMD (Mac)-D.

The Elliptical Marquee Tool

We're now going to switch gears for a little change of pace. Select the Elliptical Marquee tool, found in the same tool slot in the Tools panel as the Rectangular Marquee tool. The good news is that all of the keyboard shortcuts we've learned so far apply to the Elliptical Marquee tool as well. They also apply to every other selection tool in the Tools panel.

A couple of shortcuts are specific to both of the marquee tools, however. One is a shortcut that allows you to constrain the proportions of the width and height of the marquee tools as you create with them. To do that, hold down SHIFT. You're probably thinking, "I thought pressing SHIFT added to the existing selection area." And you're right. But to add to the selection area, you hold SHIFT *while* you click to create an additional selection. To constrain proportions, hold SHIFT *after* you create the selection. If you're adding to a selection area, you may need to release SHIFT and then press it again. Note that like the SPACEBAR shortcut, which moves selections around while you're creating them, the SHIFT key to constrain proportions also toggles this behavior. If you release the key, the proportions will not be proportional anymore. The SHIFT key forces the Elliptical Marquee tool to create perfect circles, but it also forces the Rectangular Marquee tool to create perfect squares. You also might remember that SHIFT can be used to constrain the proportions of vector shapes while you're creating them.

If you're using a keyboard shortcut to create the perfect selection, let go of your mouse button first, and then release the keyboard shortcut.

The Great Elliptical Marquee Dilemma   One of the big problems I have with the Elliptical Marquee tool is that it creates elliptical selections in the same way as the Rectangular Marquee tool creates rectangular selections: by starting at the upper-left corner. The problem is, ellipses don't have corners. So what Photoshop has to do is draw an imaginary rectangle around the ellipse, and then begin the creation (and scaling) of the ellipse from that imaginary upper-left corner. If you're confused, so am I! This is just not intuitive. If you'd like to practice with how annoying this can be, open a photo that shows someone's (or something's) eyes. Do your best to select the iris or the pupil with the Elliptical Marquee tool.

The good news is that there is a quick fix to this problem. It is the ALT (Windows)/OPT (Mac) key. As before, for this trick to work, you must hold down ALT/OPT after you start creating the selection area. What this will do (again, as long as you're holding down the key), is create the circle from its center. So, to select the iris in the *eye for practice.jpg* image, click in the center with the Elliptical Marquee tool; after clicking, hold ALT/OPT. The selection will now resize around the center, where you first clicked. That seems much more intuitive to me. As with all shortcuts we've looked at so far, this also works with the Rectangular Marquee tool.

These keyboard shortcuts are not mutually exclusive. You can scale a selection from its center and also constrain its proportions at the same time. Having the finger dexterity of a heavy-metal guitar player will make this easier, but it's still possible if you don't.

How to... Move Selections

As you start making selections, it probably won't be too long before you make the perfect selection—in the wrong spot. So, how do you move a selection area? It depends on what you want to do.

If you want to move a selection while you are in the process of creating it (in other words, if you haven't released the mouse button while dragging to create the selection), then you can hold down the SPACEBAR to move the selection area. As you've probably noticed, dragging the mouse around while creating selections will resize the selection area. But while you hold down the SPACEBAR, moving the mouse will move the selection area. Be aware that this keyboard shortcut only toggles selection movement. That means that as soon as you release the SPACEBAR, you'll be back to resizing the selection when you move your mouse.

Once you release your mouse button, the selection is made. The SPACEBAR won't help you move the selection area around at that point. To move a selection area that you've already created, first make sure that you have a selection tool (such as one of the marquee tools) selected in the Tools panel. It does not have to be the same one used to create the selection. With a selection tool selected, put your cursor inside the selection area, and your cursor will turn into a white arrow next to a tiny marquee area. You can then drag to move the selection area around.

Be careful if you have the Move tool selected. When you drag a selection with the Move tool, you'll actually move the selected pixels on the currently selected layer.

Designing with the Marquee Selection Tools

Typically, you'd want to create any type of page layout or design with the vector drawing tools because of their flexibility. But occasionally it pays to know how to do the same tricks with the marquee tools. This is also a good way to practice using Photoshop.

We're going to create the beginnings of a '50s-style album cover. We won't use a photo or text here, but you can add those later as you feel comfortable. First, let's create a new document with the default Photoshop settings. Regardless of what color your background color is, we'll make a new layer and fill it with black. To do that, make a new blank layer, and then select it. Press D on your keyboard to reset the foreground and background colors to their defaults. This will make black the foreground color. Then press the keyboard shortcut ALT-BACKSPACE (Windows)/OPT-DELETE (Mac) to fill this layer with the foreground color. We're now going to create shapes with the marquee tools, and then fill them using this shortcut.

Next, create another new layer. With the Rectangular Marquee tool selected, create a large rectangle on the left side of the document. For reference, go ahead and peek at Figure 6-7. Next, in the Color Picker, select the color **120**, **200**, **240**. With the new layer selected, fill this layer with the foreground color. Notice that the blue color only fills the selected area.

Create yet another new layer (your third new layer, if you're keeping track). Make another rectangular selection along the left edge of the last one. Make it skinnier this time. With the empty new layer selected, fill it with a lighter blue color with the RGB values **190**, **220**, **240**.

Finally, select the Elliptical Marquee tool in the Tools panel. Make one last blank new layer. This time make an elliptical marquee selection on the left side of the document, but make it so that the left half of the selection is off the edge of the document. If you need a refresher on how to move selections, check out the sidebar earlier in this chapter. We're going to fill this shape with the color **120**, **80**, **120**. Now the skeleton of our album cover is in place (see Figure 6-7). From here we

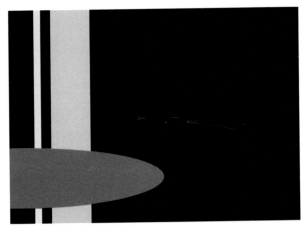

FIGURE 6-7 The completed album cover layout design

could add layer styles to these individual shapes, add text, add a background image, and so on.

 You can also use selection tools to delete pixels by selecting them and pressing DELETE on your keyboard.

The Lasso Tools

We're now going to look at the selection tools that you'll find below the marquee tools in the Tools panel. These are the lasso tools. Since we already know how to create, deselect, add, subtract, move, and use selections, we'll go through these tools much more quickly.

The Lasso Tool

The Lasso tool is used to create freeform selections. Instead of your dragging to make a predefined shape, the Lasso tool allows you to just drag to draw a selection. Although this gives much more freedom, it can be tough to control with a mouse—at least it is for me. Using a graphics tablet can really help with the use of the Lasso tool.

With the Lasso tools, things work a little differently because you're making your own selection area. You'll notice that if you make a selection that is not a complete shape—say, for example, a single curve like the letter *C*—then Photoshop will automatically draw a line back to the starting point for you. This is because all selections must be areas that are completely enclosed. You can't have a selection line. Remember that we're selecting groups of pixels in a closed area, so lines just won't cut it.

The Polygonal Lasso Tool

The Polygonal Lasso is used for manually creating selections that don't have curves. It works differently from what we've seen before. There isn't any dragging, only clicking. You click to create points (as shown in Figure 6-8), and when you're done, click the starting point again.

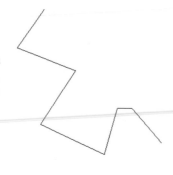

FIGURE 6-8 This is what it looks like when you're creating a selection with the Polygonal Lasso tool.

If you want to create a curvy line while you're using the Polygonal Lasso tool, hold the ALT (Windows)/OPT (Mac) key, and while you do, you'll be temporarily using the regular Lasso tool. Release ALT/OPT to get back to the Polygonal Lasso tool.

The Magnetic Lasso Tool

The most intelligent of the selection tools we've looked at so far, the Magnetic Lasso tries to help you make your selections. It does this by looking for areas of contrast and guessing where you want to make a selection.

FIGURE 6-9 The Magnetic Lasso tool tries to follow the edges between contrasting colors.

To practice this, again open the *eye for practice.jpg* image. This image is a great candidate for use of the Magnetic Lasso tool. There is good contrast on the left side of the image. The boy's hair is dark, and the background to the left of that is much lighter. To select the background area, just click at the top of the image between the hair and the background with the Magnetic Lasso tool. Let go of the mouse button and drag the mouse down loosely, and even if your cursor doesn't remain precisely on the edge, the Magnetic Lasso tool will try its best to cling to that edge where the contrast is greatest, as shown in Figure 6-9.

Just be aware that not everything is good for using the Magnetic Lasso tool. If you have an image of a car on a city street and you want to select the car to move it to another image, you will probably have a tough time with the tires. Usually a lot of shadows are around tires in photos. You may be able to easily discern where the tire should stop and the street should start, but the Magnetic Lasso tool may not have the same skill.

The Quick Selection Tool

The Quick Selection tool is like an automatic Magnetic Lasso tool in the form of a brush. Just drag in an area, and the Quick Selection tool guesses what you want selected. The good part (for beginners) and the bad part (for experts) is that this tool doesn't offer any other controls or real options to control how it selects what it does. Luckily, it usually does pretty well on the first try.

To practice with this tool, I'm going to open the file *selecting tulip.jpg*. Feel free to use your own image to follow along. To use the Quick Selection tool, I'll simply drag around

FIGURE 6-10 Drag around the image's background to select the background.

the background of the tulip that is shown in Figure 6-10. Just a large sweeping motion is fine; no need to move your cursor to the edges. If it's taking you longer than 3 or 4 seconds on an image like this, you're probably putting more effort into it than you need to. If you missed a spot, you can just click it to add it to the selection area. The Quick Selection tool doesn't need a shortcut in order to add to the selection area. If the tool selects too much, as with other selection tools, hold the ALT (Windows)/OPT (Mac) key to click or paint out areas you don't want selected.

Note We'll talk in the next chapter about how to edit images and make changes to color and other attributes of images, or changes to selected areas of images.

Selecting by Color

Instead of manually selecting pixels, we can also select pixels based on their color. This can really help in a variety of circumstances. Let's say you're trying to select something like wispy hair blowing in the wind. It would be a nearly impossible task using the lasso or marquee tools. But selecting by color can pick up some of the subtleties (such as feathered edges) that would be otherwise impossible with the selection tools we've looked at so far.

FIGURE **6-11** The *Magic Wand Practice.psd* file

The Magic Wand Tool

The Magic Wand tool selects by color. You'll find it in the same tool slot in the Tools panel as the Quick Selection tool. The Magic Wand tool is simple enough to use, but it has some quirks. I've created a simple Photoshop document that exploits these quirks. This document basically contains a few layers with circles on them (see Figure 6-11). I can simply click a circle once to select the entire thing. This is because all colors that are both similar and next to the one you clicked are selected.

Tip   In a real-world scenario, you wouldn't have to use the Magic Wand or any other tool to select these circles. To select objects that are on their own layer, simply hold the CTRL (Windows)/CMD (Mac) key while clicking the layer's thumbnail in the Layers panel. Everything on the layer will instantly be selected.

When you click a blank layer with the Magic Wand tool, things don't always work correctly. This is because the default settings for the Magic Wand tool only allow it to "see" the objects on the currently selected layer. To allow it to see all layers at once, I will select the Sample All Layers check box in the Options bar. Now when I click one of the green circles, it is selected. As with other selection tools, you can hold SHIFT or ALT/OPT to add to or subtract from the current selection. So, for example, if you want to select a shirt that someone is wearing and the shirt was red and purple, you can click the red, and then SHIFT-click (hold SHIFT while clicking) the purple spots.

But what if there were multiple people with red and purple shirts? Wouldn't it be just the coolest thing if we could select them all at once? There is a way to do that, and it is by deselecting the Contiguous option in the Options bar. You can try it in the Magic Wand Practice document you have open. Once you deselect Contiguous (which means "touching"), then the Magic Wand tool will select all of the pixels of that color in the entire document, not just the pixels that are similar and touching the area you clicked.

You can also fine-tune the Magic Wand tool by using the Tolerance option in the Options bar. The Tolerance option determines how many colors similar to the one you clicked are selected. If you find that the Magic Wand tool is selecting too many colors, reduce the Tolerance value. If it's not selecting enough variations of the color you're clicking, increase the Tolerance value. If it helps you remember, think of the Tolerance value like tolerance in people; if they're very tolerant, they're accepting of more people. If they're intolerant, they aren't as welcoming.

 The Magic Wand tool is notorious for creating aliased, or hard-edged, selections (even if Anti-Aliased is checked in the Options bar). If you're selecting things with soft or curvy edges such as hair or grass, you're probably better off using Color Range.

Color Range

Color Range is not a tool; it's a command. It functions very similarly to the way that the Magic Wand tool does, only it typically returns much better results than the Magic Wand. But this is a very complex and powerful tool, so we'll just get the basic idea and move on.

I'll start by opening a file we've already looked at—*sea of daffodils.jpg*. Go back to Figure 6-3 if you'd like to see what this image looks like. The problem here is that pieces of the blue sky are hidden behind a lot of branches. If we wanted to select the sky to change its color (which we'll see how to do in the next chapter), we'd have a tough time with any of the selection methods we've looked at thus far. But this is a perfect job for Color Range.

Color Range selects a range of colors throughout the document. To apply it, go to the Select menu and select Color Range to open the Color Range dialog box (see Figure 6-12). Your cursor instantly turns into an eyedropper, which you'll use

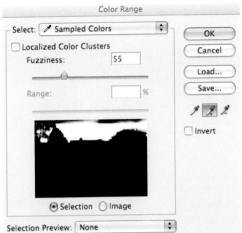

<figure>Figure 6-12 The Color Range dialog box</figure>

to select the colors you want. I'm going to go to the sky of the image with the daffodils and click in an area of blue that best represents the blue in the sky. The black-and-white representation of the image now shows white where there is sky.

White represents selected areas, and black represents areas that are not selected. You might notice some gray areas. These are pixels that are *partially* selected. Partial selection of a pixel is an advanced concept we won't get into too much in this book, but it essentially means what it sounds like. If we were to colorize a partially selected pixel, it would only be partially colorized.

You can use the + and − eyedropper tools to add and remove colors from your selection. But if you just want to subtly tweak the colors already selected, adjust the Fuzziness value. The Fuzziness value is somewhat like the Tolerance value in the Magic Wand tool, except that in Color Range, you can actually see the difference it is making to the selection area.

Adjusting Selections

Often, after you've created selections, you'll find that you'd like to adjust them. In this section, we'll look at a few of the many ways to do this.

The Select Menu

The Select menu, where we found Color Range, is your one-stop shop for all things selection related. If you ever forget how to do anything pertaining to selections, you can probably find your answers by using this menu. The two options you should be aware of from this menu are Inverse and Reselect.

Inverse deselects everything that is currently selected and selects everything that is currently deselected. Let's say that we want to select the tulip instead of the background in the *selecting tulip.jpg* image we looked at earlier in this chapter. Perhaps it's easier to select the background than the tulip. No worries. Just select the background, and then choose Select | Inverse to select the tulip.

Reselect will select whatever you had selected last. This is very handy for those times when you've deselected and then performed a few extra steps that you don't want to undo, but you want your selection back. Choose Select | Reselect to select whatever was selected last.

Tip You can also save a selection from this menu. The selection will save with your document, and you can reload it anytime from the Select menu. This is great for complicated selections that take a while to create.

Refine Edge

When you've met two conditions, you will have access to the very powerful Refine Edge dialog box. The two conditions are these: you must have a currently active selection, and you must have a selection tool selected. Do those two things, and the Refine Edge button will be clickable in the Options bar.

The Refine Edge dialog box allows you much more control over how your selection works. As you can see from Figure 6-13, it has some very helpful options. The first two options are powerful, but complex. You can create a rough selection of intricate objects, and then have Photoshop attempt to find the details and refine the selection for you.

The Smooth option is great for something like the Magic Wand tool, which can return rough edges. Increase the Smooth value to create a smoother transition.

The Feather option allows you to blur the edges of the selection. You can see what effect this property has on your selection by looking at the preview in the document window. Use feathering when you want to make subtle changes (such as a color change to the sky) and you want it to blend in instead of having the hard edge created by the selection.

The Contract/Expand option allows you to shrink or enlarge your selection by dragging the slider to the left or right, respectively. This is great for those times when you realize that you selected too much, or that you didn't quite get all the pixels in your selection.

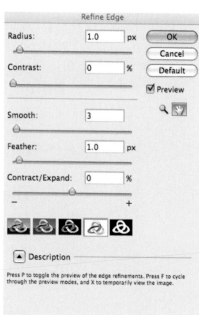

FIGURE 6-13 The Refine Edge dialog box

About Troubleshooting and Selections

Here's my greatest tip to you. I've been teaching Photoshop at all levels all over the country for almost a decade. I don't think I've ever taught a class or consulted at a company where someone didn't get stuck and couldn't figure out what was wrong. In almost all of those cases, the problem was the same—they had the wrong thing selected! I've now gotten to the point where as soon as I've heard that one of my students has an issue, my first question is "What do you have selected?" If you can't paint, it's possible that you accidentally selected a couple of pixels in another area of the document that you can't see.

This selection troubleshooting also works with layers. You might perform a command such as a color adjustment or painting, and you might not see the result of it because you don't have the right layer selected. Photoshop couldn't care less what you're looking at. All it cares about is what you have selected, with layers or with selection areas. Those are the things that we use to tell Photoshop what to edit. When something isn't behaving as expected, always ask yourself first, "What do I have selected?" You'll be amazed at the problems you solve on your own!

7

Working with Images

How to...

- Browse images with Adobe Bridge
- Edit images in Adobe Camera Raw
- Perform basic color corrections
- Use selections with image adjustments
- Crop images

To many users of Photoshop, editing photos is the most important reason for Photoshop's existence. After all, it is named *Photo*shop. So, this chapter introduces you to the world of photo editing. In the process, we'll also look at a couple of extra applications that come with Photoshop—Adobe Bridge and Camera Raw. We'll then look at image editing inside of Photoshop itself.

Browsing Images with Bridge

Some Photoshop users never know that when Photoshop is installed, so is another program called Adobe Bridge. Bridge is an application primarily used to browse files, but it does so much more than that. In addition to browsing and giving previews of images, graphics files (such as Adobe Illustrator), audio files, and video files, Bridge can also open Camera Raw, download photos from cameras connected to your computer, perform many automated tasks, color manage all applications in the entire Creative Suite that utilize color management, create slideshows, sort and organize files, and more.

For this section on Adobe Bridge, I'll be browsing the Samples folder that ships with Photoshop. These files are not included with the exercise files that accompany this book. If you'd like to browse the same files, you can navigate Bridge to Photoshop's root directory (for Windows users, this is Program Files | Adobe | Adobe Photoshop CS4; for Mac users, this is Applications | Adobe Photoshop CS4), and open the Samples folder.

Launching Bridge

To open Adobe Bridge, launch it the same way you would open any other program. Bridge is what we call a "stand-alone" application, meaning that it can be opened and used by itself, without the help of another program. Photoshop does not need to be open when you're using Bridge.

If you have Photoshop open already, you can open Bridge by going to the File menu and selecting Browse In Bridge. Once you've selected this option, have a little patience. Bridge will begin the process of opening. It can sometimes take a few moments to open, especially if it's the first time you're launching Bridge, or if Bridge is previewing a folder with many files for the first time.

 You can also open Bridge from Photoshop by using the keyboard shortcut CTRL-ALT-O (Windows)/ CMD-OPT-O (Mac), or by clicking the orange Bridge icon at the top of the interface.

Quick Tour of the Bridge Interface

Very quickly, let's go through the Bridge interface. Use Figure 7-1 as a guide as we tour the various components of the Bridge interface. If you're on Windows, your interface may look slightly different from Figure 7-1, but the differences are minor and only cosmetic.

As with Photoshop, the top bar is the Menu bar. Below the Menu bar, we have a little tool area for frequently accessed items, such as back/forward buttons, recent files, the photo downloader, and more. Immediately below the tools, we find the navigation area. This indicates where the folder you're currently looking at is located on your computer. But these folders are also buttons. In this case, if I want to go back to the root folder of Photoshop, I can just click the Adobe Photoshop CS4 folder located in the navigation area to quickly jump to that location.

The bulk of Adobe Bridge is taken up by panels, which work like the panels in Photoshop. A Favorites panel contains important locations on your hard drive that you may want to

FIGURE 7-1 The Bridge interface

jump to at some point, such as your desktop or your Documents folder. You can also drag additional folders to this area to create your own favorite locations.

The Content panel displays the files of the current folder you've navigated to. When you select a file by clicking it once, Bridge will give you a larger preview in the Preview panel, assuming that the file format is supported.

Tip It's important to click the file only once to preview it. If you double-click the thumbnail, it will open the image in Photoshop. If you open Bridge from another Adobe application, double-clicking the thumbnail will open the image in the program you used to launch Bridge (rather than in Photoshop). Genius!

The Metadata panel displays the metadata for the selected file. Metadata is a fairly new concept in image editing. *Metadata* is essentially extra data about a file, and this data is typically stored in the file itself. It's almost like you hired a private detective to find out all sorts of secret details about a file, and the resulting report is metadata. For example, if you look at the metadata for a digital photo that you took with a DSLR camera, Bridge will probably show you the aperture of the lens, the shutter speed, the ISO, the pixel dimensions, whether the flash was used, the color profile, and other details about the way the photo was taken.

You can also manually input additional metadata, such as who took the photo, their e-mail address and other contact information, and more. To put in your own metadata information, simply click across from a property to get a text field, type the information, and then press ENTER/RETURN. Pressing TAB will allow you to move from field to field to input information. Bridge also lets you input metadata for other types of files, such as audio and video files.

Browsing Files with Bridge

A couple of great features add a lot to the quality of your experience with Bridge: a slider and the Loupe tool. The little slider is at the very bottom of the interface. This slider controls the size of the thumbnails in the Content panel. As I drag this to the right, we can see the thumbnail size increase (see Figure 7-2).

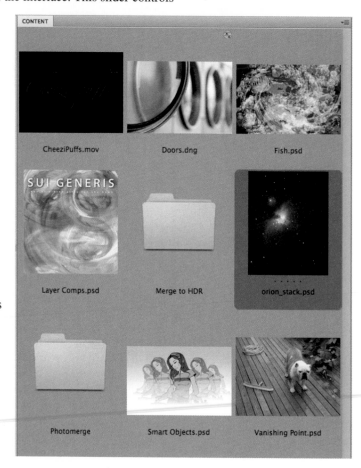

FIGURE 7-2 After increasing the size of the thumbnails

The Loupe Tool

When clicking an image once to preview it in the Preview panel, you can resize the Bridge interface (just like in Photoshop) to see a larger preview. However, this is usually not enough to see the true quality of an image. For larger images, you can only see things like subtle motion blur, compression artifacts, and other problems and details when you zoom in close.

Bridge allows you to zoom in close by using a hidden tool called the Loupe tool. Just click once to see a portion of an image close up (see Figure 7-3). You can also drag this zoom area around to zoom into

other parts of the image. Click the little *x* in the Loupe tool preview area to close it.

Searching for Images

For Mac users, this won't be very impressive, but Bridge allows you to do a speedy search for images. I've spent a lot of time on Windows machines, and one of my biggest frustrations is how time-consuming and inaccurate its file searching capabilities are. To do a Mac-style search that is incredibly fast and accurate, click in the field with the magnifying glass in the upper-right corner of the Bridge interface. Type your search terms, and press ENTER/RETURN.

FIGURE 7-3 After clicking an image in the Preview panel to zoom in with the Loupe tool

How to... Organize Images with Bridge

One of Bridge's great benefits is the way it allows you to sort and organize your files. We've already seen one way to do that when we looked at metadata. Next to the Metadata panel, you'll find the Keywords panel. You can input keywords for a selected file in this panel. Then, when doing searches in Bridge (which you can do from the search field, or by going to Edit | Find), you can search based on the keywords you've input. You can even create keyword categories. Let's say you've created a Food category. You can select a photo of spaghetti, and assign the Food category to this image. Then when you do a search on "Food," this image will show up in the search results, because that is the keyword that you assigned to it.

You can also rank and label files in Bridge. To rank a file, increase the size of its thumbnail until it is fairly large. Then click it once to select it. If the thumbnail is large enough, you'll see five little dots above the name of the image. You can click one of these

(continued)

dots to give it a rank. So, if you click on the second dot from the left, you'll be giving it a rank of 2 stars. If you right-click an image, you can also assign a label to it, such as "Approved" or "Review." Thus, when you come back to this image later, you will instantly know what is going on with this image in terms of your workflow.

In the upper-right corner of the Bridge interface, you'll see a little star drop-down. From this drop-down, you can select how to view files. This star drop-down acts as a filter. Let's say you only want to look at images that you've ranked as 4 or 5 stars; from the star drop-down, you would select Show 4 Or More Stars. You can also select to show only labeled items. Next to the star drop-down is another drop-down that controls how images are sorted and displayed. By default, images are displayed by filename. But you can change this drop-down so that files are sorted and displayed by the size of the file, the last time it was modified, its birthday (date of creation), or other factors. Using these tools in Bridge can really help you get a handle on a large collection of files.

Editing Images in Camera Raw

Even if you never use Camera Raw, we're going to use it as a tool to learn the basic concepts of image editing. With increasing frequency, when I just want to adjust color or brightness for an entire image, I find myself doing those tasks in Camera Raw rather than in Photoshop. Camera Raw is so powerful yet so simple and intuitive.

Did You Know?

What "Raw" Means

The purpose of Camera Raw is to adjust digital negative, or "raw," files. These are unprocessed files taken with a higher-end digital camera. Most of the time when images are taken with a digital camera, these images are processed and converted to a file format such as JPEG or TIFF. Raw files are not processed and allow you to do the processing.

The benefit of raw image files is that editing usually looks much better than with a processed file such as a JPEG or a TIFF. The downside is that these files are usually in the proprietary raw format of your camera and must be taken into a program like Photoshop and converted to a more common file format before sharing. Raw image files are also significantly larger than JPEG or even TIFF files.

I prefer to shoot in raw as much as I can. I never know when I'm going to take a photo that I'll want to keep around forever or that I just absolutely love. It drives me nuts when I can't precisely replicate a beautiful photo, like one of my children making a funny face or a gorgeous sunset that I shot as a JPEG to save disc space. I work so much in Photoshop that it's not an inconvenience to import the raw files and convert them to another format for sharing. But that's just my preference.

 In the latest versions of Camera Raw, JPEG and TIFF files can also be edited.

Getting Images into Camera Raw

The quickest and easiest way to get images into the Camera Raw application is from Adobe Bridge. If the image is a JPEG or a TIFF file, right-click the image in Bridge and select Open In Camera Raw. If the image is a raw image, you only have to double-click it to open Camera Raw.

 Photoshop recognizes a wide range of proprietary raw image files from all of the common digital camera manufacturers. If you purchase a new camera and its raw format is not supported by Camera Raw, check for Photoshop updates, which will likely have the fix.

In Bridge, I'm going to navigate to a file called *Butterfly.dng*, and then double-click it to open Camera Raw. This file is in the DNG (digital negative format) created by Adobe to be a standard raw file format. I really like this image as it is already, but we're going to edit this image and have some fun with the colors in it.

 You can select multiple images in Bridge and open all of them in Camera Raw at once. You can also select multiple images at once in Camera Raw, allowing you to perform the same adjustments on multiple images at the same time. This is really useful for photo shoots where every photo turned out too dark, or too warm, and so forth.

Editing in Camera Raw

Editing images in Camera Raw takes place in a series of tabs (like the panels in Photoshop) on the right side of the Camera Raw interface.

Enabling Clipping Warnings

Before getting started with editing, it's a really good idea to be aware of the clipping warnings and how to turn them on and off. In the upper-right corner of the Camera Raw dialog box, you'll see something called a *histogram* (see Figure 7-4). It's a graph that gives you a live update of the colors and brightness in your image.

FIGURE 7-4 The Camera Raw histogram and clipping warning switches

The upper-left and upper-right corners of the histogram each contain a triangle. The one on the left turns on the *shadow* clipping warnings, while the one on the right turns on the *highlight* clipping warnings. Go ahead and click both of them to turn them on. If they get too annoying, you can click them again to turn them back off. But these little annoyances are actually lifesavers. They indicate when the brights are getting too bright and when the shadows are getting too dark.

When shadows and highlights are clipped, the result is something called *posterization*. In the image editing business, posterization is the visual equivalent of a pothole, and it's just as painful to encounter. It means that a hard edge exists between colors that should have a smooth transition. So, when you have shadow areas that are being crunched to pure black, Camera Raw will turn those pixels an obvious and ugly blue to let you know. When detail is being lost in highlight areas, those pixels will turn red to so indicate.

Camera Raw's Basic Tab

We'll now embark on another mini-project with this butterfly image. We'll start in the Basic tab in Camera Raw. The Basic tab contains the essential image-editing parameters—exposure, contrast, saturation, and so on.

The first slider we come to is for Temperature, which we covered earlier in Chapter 4. By dragging this slider to the left, you can add a cool color tint to this image; dragging to the right creates a warm color tint.

We'll now jump to the Exposure property. Exposure on a camera is created by opening the aperture, which allows more light to enter the camera's lens, creating a brighter image. Increase the Exposure value to **+ 0.85**. This will overexpose (over brighten) the image, and you'll notice some ugly red pixels (see Figure 7-5). This shows our highlight clipping warning in full effect, letting us know that these pixels are too bright and that we're losing detail in these highlight areas.

Camera Raw has a nifty feature that allows you to restore these failing highlight areas while still keeping most of the brightness added by increasing the Exposure value. That feature is the next slider, Recovery. I'm going to increase the Recovery value to about 70. That does diminish some of the brightness that we added, but it still looks brighter than the original. To compare the before and after of all changes made in this

FIGURE 7-5 These red pixels indicate overexposure.

area, press P key on your keyboard, which shows you the image before edits. Press P again to see the image after edits.

If you want to add more light to the midtone areas—the areas that don't qualify as shadows or highlights—you can increase the Fill Light property. Increasing the Blacks value will darken the shadow areas. Be careful with this, though. Increasing this value too much will create clipping in the shadow areas of the image. I will also increase the Contrast value to +30 to add more brightness to lighter areas and less brightness to darker areas.

> **Tip** Increasing contrast is especially beneficial for images that need to look intense, or even iconic, such as movie posters, art for rock bands, and so on.

Next, we come to the Clarity value. This is similar to sharpening; it adds more clarity to details in the image. Decreasing the Clarity value blurs the image. I increased the Clarity value a little, to about +20.

Then we have the Vibrance and Saturation parameters, which appear at first glance to do the same thing. However, the Vibrance value will also increase and decrease color intensity, as does Saturation, except that Vibrance has respect for skin tones. If you have a photo with people that have Caucasian skin tones and you increase Saturation, the people will soon turn Oompa Loompa orange. Increasing Vibrance will limit how vibrant the skin tones are allowed to go so that the saturation added maintains a natural look. For now, I'm not going to touch Vibrance or Saturation because we're about to look at a way to adjust image color that allows for more control.

The HSL/Grayscale Tab

Let's now skip over to the HSL/Grayscale tab on the right side of the Camera Raw interface. This tab allows for control over individual colors.

 Tip   To create a black-and-white image, select the Convert To Grayscale option at the top of the HSL/Grayscale tab.

You'll see that within the HSL/Grayscale tab are three more tabs—Hue, Saturation, and Luminance. This is for adjusting the hue, saturation, and lightness of each of the individual colors listed below. Let's start by adjusting the red color on the butterfly's wing. In the Hue tab, adjust the red color by dragging the Reds value to the right. This turns the red color on the butterfly's wing into orange. No selection needed! Also, nothing else in the image is changed.

Let's keep this party going by changing the Hue value of green to more of a blue/green. To do this, drag the Greens slider to the right. Finally, change the hue of the flowers by adjusting the Purples value. I dragged it to the right to create magenta-tinted flowers (see Figure 7-6). And so we see the power of the Hue tab in Camera Raw—we can change colors into other colors adjacent to them on the color wheel.

FIGURE 7-6 The butterfly so far

Tip As grass dies, it becomes more yellow. The opposite of yellow is blue, so if you want to make grass look more vibrant and alive, add a little blue, as we did here.

I like how this image is turning out, but it's a little (okay, a lot) overdone. The colors have now gone from beautiful to cartoony and fake looking. That happens sometimes as you're adjusting hue in Camera Raw. This is because some colors are just brighter than others. It's not really a big deal because we can just hop on over to the Saturation and Luminance tabs to polish this up. First, let's see the Saturation tab.

Let's start on the left side of the image, with the red (now orange) spot that appears to be glowing. I'm going to take the value for the saturation of the Reds down to about –40. I'm also going to take the Greens to about –20. Finally, I'll take the Purples to –40 to mellow out the flowers a little. This is starting to look more believable, but the flowers are still too intense. However, it's not the amount of color that's making them too intense, it's their brightness. So, let's go over to the Luminance tab to fix this.

In the Luminance tab, I'll take the luminance of the Purples down to about –50 or so. This will darken only the purple colors in the image (see Figure 7-7). Reducing the luminance of colors can play a large role in getting the colors you want. Oftentimes,

FIGURE 7-7 The adjusted butterfly image

when you're color correcting a sky, for example, changing the hue doesn't make that much of a difference because the sky is too bright. In those cases, it's often best to reduce the brightness of the sky to bring color back in and then to adjust the hue.

Getting Images Out of Camera Raw

Once you're done editing your image in Camera Raw (often abbreviated as ACR, for Adobe Camera Raw), you have several choices. In the bottom right corner of the Camera Raw interface, you'll see three buttons: Open Image, Cancel, and Done. Clicking Open Image will open this image in Photoshop for further editing. Clicking the Cancel button will cancel all changes. Clicking the Done button will close Camera Raw but will save your changes. The original butterfly image will remain untouched. Bridge stores the changes you made, so it *looks* like you've adjusted your image, but really Bridge is storing the changes you've made to your image as metadata. At any time, you can open the image back up in Camera Raw and make more changes, or take things back to their defaults.

Converting Images in Camera Raw

In the bottom left corner of Camera Raw is a Save Image button. Clicking this button will open a dialog box that will allow you to save the raw file in a different file format. This is helpful when you would like to quickly convert a file to a different file format for sharing.

 At the bottom of the Camera Raw interface is blue text that contains technical info about your image. You can click the text to open a dialog box that will allow you to change details about your image such as resolution and size.

Basic Image Editing in Photoshop

Now that we know a little bit about image editing, let's get into Photoshop and see how to perform similar adjustments there.

The Adjustments Panel

The workflow for color adjustments has changed in Photoshop CS4. The Adjustments panel is now the only place you need to go to find color adjustments.

The Adjustments panel is a very intuitive panel, except for the icons. If you just hold your mouse over the icons, a little pop-up will indicate the adjustment that will be created by clicking that button. To practice adding adjustments from this panel, I will open the file *Space Needle.psd,* shown in Figure 7-8. You'll probably want to open up a dark image of your own to work

FIGURE 7-8 The original space needle image

100%   Doc: 3.60M/3.60M

along with me. These concepts are pretty abstract to just read about and will make much more sense when you actually perform these steps yourself.

As you can see, this image is way too dark, so we're going to correct this by applying a Levels adjustment. To do this, click the icon on the top row of adjustments, second from the left. The icon looks like fire with three triangles underneath it (it's actually not fire, as you'll see in a moment). Once you click the icon, Photoshop will create an *adjustment* layer. This is a separate "layer" that applies the selected adjustment to all objects below it in the layer stack in the Layers panel. You can test this by dragging layers on top of the adjustment layer. Once you do, they will no longer be affected by the adjustment layer.

In addition to creating an adjustment layer, once you click the Levels icon in the Adjustments panel, the Adjustments panel changes to show you the options for the Levels adjustment. We see here another histogram with three triangles underneath. So, what is a histogram exactly? A *histogram* displays the quantity of all brightness levels in an image. Dark shadow values are represented on the left of the histogram; bright highlight values are represented on the right of the histogram. So, in the Space Needle image, a big spike is on the left side of the histogram, which indicates a lot of that particular shadow value. The right side of the histogram is just blank, which indicates that there are no bright values at all. Looking at the image confirms this.

We can brighten images by using the triangle underneath the highlights. Drag it to the left until it is under the first pixels in the histogram (see Figure 7-9). This will force the area with those first pixels to become bright, resulting in a significant lightening of the image.

FIGURE 7-9 The Levels adjustment after brightening the highlights

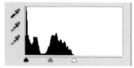

The white triangle adjusts highlights. The black triangle adjusts shadow areas. The gray triangle lightens and darkens the midtone values of the image, while maintaining highlights and shadows.

You can continue adding adjustments by going back to the Adjustments panel. The way to get back to all the icons is by clicking the arrow button at the bottom left corner of the Adjustments panel.

Here's a summary of some of the most common adjustments, from top to bottom, left to right:

- **Brightness/Contrast**   Only adjusts brightness and contrast. No control over highlights, shadows, or midtones. Very limited, but also very simple and easy to use.

- **Levels**   More advanced luminance correction. Much more powerful and complex than Brightness/Contrast, but also has a much steeper learning curve.

- **Curves**   The most powerful of all luminance correctors, but also the most challenging to master.

- **Exposure**   Like exposure on a camera. Adds/removes light. Pretty easy to use.

- **Vibrance**   A new adjustment in Photoshop CS4, this allows you to apply only vibrance and saturation, as in the Basic tab of Camera Raw.

- **Hue/Saturation**   Perhaps my favorite color adjustment. Very simple and straightforward. Similar to the HSL/Grayscale tab in Camera Raw.

- **Black & White**   Used for powerful conversion from color to black and white. Black & White allows you to control the shade of gray that colors convert to.

- **Invert**   Inverts colors. This is good if you want to turn white to black, or black to white, or if you want to make a scary image out of a photograph.

- **Threshold**   Turns every pixel pure black or pure white. It's great for turning photos into edgy street art or art for punk bands (think of the cover of Rancid's *...And Out Come the Wolves*).

 All adjustments in the Adjustments panel are nondestructive, meaning that they don't permanently change the pixels in an image. You can turn off the visibility of the adjustment layer, double-click its icon to change the values, or even delete the adjustment layer. Adjustment layers preserve your pixels from the damage of permanent change.

Limiting Adjustments with Selections

Using selections, we can control which portions of the images are affected by color adjustments. Previously, we looked at how to use the intelligence of Photoshop to avoid having to select areas of color we want to adjust. This worked well when we were looking at the HSL/Grayscale tab's color-correction features. Hue/Saturation in Photoshop has similar color-selection capabilities. We can use selections to create some cool effects that Camera Raw and Hue/Saturation on their own can't do.

In the following project, we'll take a regular image and add some color adjustments to create large dark areas. This is a common technique used to create posters and other designs based on a single image. You can then place text (which we'll cover in a later chapter) onto the dark areas, and the text will stand out more. As before, it is recommended that you use an image of your own to follow along with me.

Using the *Space Needle.psd* image, I will create a rectangular selection that goes from the top of the image to the bottom, and

FIGURE 7-10 The Space Needle image after making a selection and then applying an adjustment

that goes through the center of the Space Needle. What we want to create is a single strip of color, with black-and-white pixels on either side of it. The strip we've selected is perfect as is, but we need to change the rest of the image. For that, we need to invert the selection. Invert the selection by going to the Select menu and choosing Inverse.

Now, we can add an adjustment. When you create an adjustment while you have an active selection, the adjustment will only apply to the selected area. Even if you go back and change the adjustment later, it will still only affect the pixels in the area that was selected when you first applied the adjustment. So, apply a Hue/Saturation adjustment. Take the Saturation value down all the way to the left. You can also take down the Lightness value a little for added effect if you want. Figure 7-10 shows the final result.

Cropping Images

We're going to finish out this chapter on editing images by shifting gears a bit and looking at cropping. Cropping images is the process of making an image smaller by eliminating pieces of it that you don't want. We can use cropping to focus our viewers' attention on the things that we want them to focus on. We'll now crop this Space Needle image to create a greater focus on the important parts.

To crop, select the Crop tool in the Tools panel (underneath the Quick Selection tool). Then drag in the document window as you would with a marquee selection tool. You then get a crop preview window, which you can adjust to your liking by dragging the little boxes on the edges and at the corners. Everything that will be deleted and cropped is outside of the box and is darkened. When you're ready to make the crop, press ENTER/RETURN. For this image, I wanted to get rid of some of the junk on the top and bottom of the image, and I wanted to center the Space Needle a bit more. You might want to crop out the building on the right, but I'm going to keep it because I dig its texture. Figure 7-11 shows the image after the crop.

FIGURE 7-11 The final Space Needle image, after all adjustments and cropping

8

Blending Layers

How to...

- Combine multiple images
- Blend layers using blend modes
- Non-destructively mask portions of a layer
- Adjust layer masks

Now that we have a good portion of the basics of Photoshop behind us, it's time to dig a little deeper into what layers can do. In this chapter, we'll look at ways to combine multiple images into the same document and blend them together.

You might have noticed back in Chapter 5 that while I spoke a lot about painting, I didn't mention much about erasing. Photoshop has an Eraser tool in the Tools panel that I never use because there's a much better way to erase pixels. The better way to erase is by using layer masks, which we will also cover in this chapter. This method of "erasing" hides not only pixels, but also data on vector layers and color adjustment layers. However, the best part of layer masks (in contrast to erasing with the Eraser tool) is that erased/hidden pixels can be restored at any time.

Combining Images

Before we talk about blending layers together, we need to combine images into the same Layers panel, which puts them into the same Photoshop document (PSD) file. Then you can really explore the power of layer blending. Photoshop has a couple of different ways to combine images into the same document, and you can choose which method is best for you.

Copy and Paste

The good old copy/paste maneuver even works with the combining of images. But before we combine images, we need to have them open. So, I have two images open here, *Houses at sunset.psd* and *Trees at sunset.psd*. To get the most out of this exercise, you should also open two images of your own.

When opening files, you can hold down the CTRL (Windows)/CMD (Mac) key to click multiple files to select at one time. Click Open and they will all be opened in their own tab. I'm going to click the tab with the *Trees at sunset.psd* image. Next, I'll press CTRL-A (Windows)/CMD-A (Mac) to quickly select the entire document. Then I will press the platform standard copy shortcut, CTRL-C (Windows)/CMD-C (Mac), to copy the image. Finally, I'm going to click the tab for the *Houses at sunset.psd* image and press CTRL-V (Windows)/CMD-V (Mac) to paste the trees on top of the houses. I can double-check my copying and pasting by looking at the names of my layers. I can tell I did it correctly because I'm viewing the *Houses at sunset .psd* tab, but I'm seeing trees. This is because the layer with the trees is on top of the layer with the houses (see Figure 8-1).

FIGURE 8-1 The trees pasted on top of the houses.

Dragging Layers

Don't get me wrong, I really like the new tabbed document feature of Photoshop CS4. But it does make combining files a little more annoying. Before Photoshop CS4, documents were all just floating windows. It was a mess. But the benefit was that you could easily drag layers between documents.

With Photoshop CS4, you'll need to first "untab" your document by turning it into a floating window before dragging. To do that, drag the name of the tab (*Trees at sunset.psd*, in my case) down a little. Semitransparent overlays will indicate that you are about to create a floating panel with your document.

Once you go back and click a tabbed document in the main Photoshop window, your floating document will disappear. If you have floating panels that disappear, you can retrieve them by going to the Window menu and dragging the hidden document from the bottom of the menu.

Once you've created a floating window with your document, you can drag whatever layer you select from the floating document to the tabbed document. Make sure the Move tool is selected in the Tools panel. When dragging, you will get a little box around your cursor that represents the boundaries of the layer you're moving. This allows you to place the layer you're moving wherever you'd like. However, in my case, I want this document to be centered on the *House at sunset.psd* document. To center a layer when dragging, hold down SHIFT while dragging.

Blending Images

Now that we've got two images on separate layers in the same document, we're ready to open the proverbial treasure chest that image blending represents. At first, this may seem like we're only referring to fading the top image so that the image below can show through. But we've already talked about how to do that by adjusting layer opacity. What we're going to talk about now goes far deeper, is much more powerful, and yields much more stellar results. We're now going to look at several ways to blend images together. It's good to be aware of all of the options here because all have a time and a place to be used and their own strengths and weaknesses.

This process of combining images is also referred to as "compositing" in some circles.

Layer Blend Modes

Perhaps the most common way of blending layers and the method that can potentially yield the most spectacular results is using something called layer *blend modes.* Blend modes are built into the Layers panel and can be accessed by the drop-down that reads "Normal" by default (see Figure 8-2). When you have a layer selected in the Layers panel, you can change this drop-down to control how layers interact (aka "blend") with the other layers beneath them.

FIGURE 8-2 The layer blend mode drop-down list in the Layers panel

If you click this drop-down, you'll see a list that's quite long and, with names like Linear Dodge (Add), maybe just a little intimidating. Thankfully, Adobe has provided horizontal dividers that group these blend modes into logical categories, as you can see in Figure 8-3. Think of those horizontal dividers as those rubber things at the grocery store checkout that divide other people's groceries from yours.

At the top, we have Normal and Dissolve. In Normal mode, all pixels behave as they should. In other words, nothing happens. Everything behaves normally, hence the name. In Dissolve mode, the pixels are randomly thrown out as you decrease the opacity value for the layer. Figure 8-4 shows my document with the top layer in the Dissolve blend mode and the opacity value at 50%. As you can see, some blend modes aren't useful in every situation. Because of blend modes like Dissolve, we'll just be going through the "greatest hits" of the blend modes.

FIGURE 8-3 A list of all of the blend modes, categorized by horizontal divider lines.

The "Darkening" Modes

The first category of blend modes we come to (moving from top to bottom in the blend mode drop-down), is what I call the darkening modes. These modes completely remove white pixels from the blend layer (the layer that you're changing the blend mode of) and also darken the final result.

FIGURE 8-4 The Dissolve blend mode with the layer opacity set to 50%

The most-used mode in this category is Multiply. It's the default Photoshop blend mode for shadows. Figure 8-5 shows my images with the Trees layer (the one on top) in the Multiply blend mode. Notice how the entire image is now very dark (I even had to lighten Figure 8-5 a little so that it would show up when printed in this book). Also, the light sky that was on the Trees layer has been almost completely removed. It appears as if we shot a dark nighttime photo with trees and a house. And yet this is all digital fakery at

FIGURE 8-5 The result of putting the Trees layer in the Multiply blend mode

FIGURE 8-6 The Trees layer with the Screen blend mode

its finest, especially because it took almost no effort on our part—no time-consuming selections, no destructive erasing—just a blend mode.

The "Lightening" Modes

I nicknamed the next group of blend modes the lightening modes because they basically do the opposite of the darkening modes. They lighten the final result and completely remove black. Screen is the lightening equivalent of Multiply. It's the default blend mode for glows and highlights in Photoshop. Figure 8-6 shows the result of putting the Trees layer into the Screen blend mode.

At first glance, this may appear to be similar to what you would see if you were to lower the opacity of the Trees layer and fade it into the layer of houses beneath it. But let me point out some significant differences here. First of all, the end result is lighter than either of the two layers that are being blended together. Lowering opacity can make the image lighter than the blend layer (if the layers below it are lighter), but it can't make the blend layer lighter than all of the layers below it. Another aspect of this is that pure black is completely removed from the layer in the Screen blend mode.

Look closely at Figure 8-6. The trees are actually holes on the Trees layer. This is because they were black, and the Screen blend mode completely removed them. The layer of houses beneath the Trees layer is actually very dark, so the darkness we're seeing is from the houses, not from the trees. Think of the possibilities! If you had a NASA photograph of a planet in space, the Screen blend mode would allow you to remove the blackness of outer space, leaving only planets and stars.

The "Overlay" Modes

Now things start getting interesting. The next group of blend modes is referred to as the overlay modes. The behaviors of these blend modes are a little more complicated than just darkening and lightening. These modes typically knock out 50% gray (the exact shade of gray between white and black) and add contrast by increasing the brightness of light colors and decreasing the lightness of dark colors. The overlay blend modes are great for overlaying a texture over an image.

The images of the trees and houses we've been looking at so far won't really help us to adequately illustrate the overlay blend modes, so I'm going to open a couple of new ones and combine them into the same document. Figures 8-7 and 8-8 show the two images we'll now be looking at. One is a rock pattern from Photoshop, and the other is a photo of some fish.

Next, I'm going to combine the fish photo with the rock pattern on the top layer. This rock pattern is a perfect candidate for the overlay blend modes because it has a good balance of highlights, shadows, and midtones (everything in between). For the top layer, I'm applying the Overlay blend mode. Notice how the final result looks like fish swimming in a pool of rocks (see Figure 8-9).

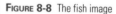

FIGURE 8-7 The rock pattern

FIGURE 8-8 The fish image

The other overlay blend modes perform similarly to Overlay. Soft Light is a more subtle effect, Hard Light is a more intense effect, and so forth.

FIGURE 8-9 The result of putting the pattern into Overlay mode

The Psychedelic Modes

The next group of blend modes creates psychedelic effects. See Figure 8-10 for what the Difference blend mode does when used to blend these images together. The results are often beautiful, but also unpredictable. The Exclusion blend mode is similar to Difference, only more washed out.

How to...   **Edit Images Instantly**

You can create some beautiful (and near-instantaneous) results from a single image, just by duplicating a layer and putting the duplicate on top in a blend mode.

First, duplicate the layer. You can do this with the keyboard shortcut CTRL-J (Windows)/ CMD-J (Mac), or you can drag a layer to the Create A New Layer button at the bottom of the Layers panel. Then put the top copy into the Overlay blend mode. Voilà! Your image will receive an instant makeover, complete with increased contrast and more vibrant color. If the effect is too intense, you can try the Soft Light blend mode. If it's still too intense, you can lower the opacity of the top layer.

The Color Utility Modes

I call the final group of blend modes the color utility modes. These are mainly utilitarian in purpose and allow you to combine color attributes of one layer (such as saturation) with the layers beneath them.

One of the things that this helps with is colorizing images. Let's say I open a black-and-white image and I want to add some color to it. So, I create a new blank layer and add some paint. The results look hideous (see Figure 8-11).

The ugly results of our painting go away when we change the blend mode to Color (see Figure 8-12). This causes the paint layer to change the color of only the layer beneath it, and the

Aligning Layers with Difference

Granted, the Difference blend mode is a little weird, but it also has great utility. If you duplicate a layer and put the duplicate in the Difference blend mode, it will turn completely black. If you move the top layer just a little, you will see small areas of color. This can be a great way to align objects. If you want identical objects on two layers to line up, put the top one in the Difference blend mode temporarily, and move the top layer until it turns black over the layer beneath it.

FIGURE 8-11 Painting on a layer above a black-and-white image looks awful.

texture of the blend layer is completely lost. This trick allows us to bring some color to colorless images.

 The Color blend mode is also great for those times when you need to demonstrate a product in a variety of different colors, but only have one photo.

FIGURE 8-12 With the paint layer in Color mode, the paint strokes colorize the image beneath it.

Layer Masks

As mentioned earlier in this chapter, layer masks are the thinking person's eraser tool. By using layer masks, we can temporarily erase portions of an image. If at any time we decide we want to restore the portions that we've hidden, we can get those pixels back.

I'm going to open two fireworks images, shown in Figures 8-13 and 8-14. I'll use layer masks to "erase" portions of the top layer of fireworks to reveal the layer of fireworks beneath it. This will result in the illusion that there were actually more fireworks, which is always a good thing.

FIGURE 8-13 The first fireworks image

Creating a Layer Mask

To create a layer mask, select the layer that you want to add the mask on, and click the Add Layer Mask button at the bottom of the Layers panel. The icon looks like a square with a circle on the inside of it. After clicking the icon and adding the layer mask, nothing much should happen, other than that the layer will have a little chain icon and a white square next to it. If you want to delete a layer mask, right-click it and select Delete Layer Mask. You can also drag the layer mask to the trash can at the bottom of the Layers panel to delete it.

FIGURE 8-14 The second
fireworks image.

 If you create a layer mask while you have an active selection, the layer mask will be created
with the selected areas already masked out.

Masking Areas on a Layer

That white square next to the layer represents the mask applied
to the layer. White areas on the mask indicate areas where the
layer is allowed to be visible. If we were to paint with black
on the mask, it would appear to erase the layer because black
pixels on the mask indicate hidden areas. Are you ready for a
bombshell? Areas that are gray indicate pixels that are *partially*
masked out. So if you painted the entire layer with 50% gray, it
would be akin to taking the opacity of the layer to 50%.

We're now going to paint on the layer mask. Select
the Brush tool in the Tools panel, and select black as your
foreground color.

Remember that pressing D resets the foreground and background colors to their defaults
(black and white), and pressing X swaps the foreground and background colors. These
shortcuts really come in handy when you're painting on layer masks.

Before painting on the mask, you need to make sure that the mask is selected. Select the mask by clicking its thumbnail in the Layers panel. It should have tiny brackets on its corners to indicate that it is selected. If you click the layer thumbnail, the layer will be selected, and painting with black will actually paint with black, instead of hiding pixels.

With the mask selected, paint on the mask in the main document window with black. Although you can't see the mask in the main document window, as long as it is selected in the Layers panel, you will be painting on the mask. The black paint on the layer mask will create a hole on the layer you painted on. We'll get back to my fireworks project in a second, but for a more obvious example of what's going on, I've created a small project with two simple layers, a blue layer on bottom, and a green layer on top. In Figure 8-15, you can see the result of painting with black on the layer mask, as well as how that looks in the Layers panel.

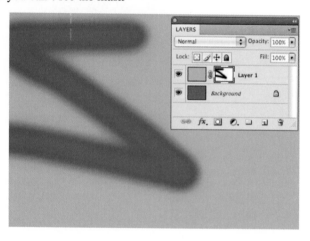

FIGURE 8-15 After painting with black on the layer mask of the green layer, we can see through to the blue layer beneath it.

The best part about layer masks is that they are completely nonpermanent. All you have to do to restore the hidden pixels is to paint with white on the layer mask! Hopefully, it makes sense now why I never use the Eraser tool, which permanently removes pixels.

Getting back to my fireworks images, I'm now going to create a mask on the top image, which is the image from Figure 8-13. This is going to blend these two layers together so that we can get the best portions of both images in one composite. Figure 8-16 shows the result after creating and painting on the layer mask of this fireworks image. This image appears courtesy of Angela McInroe.

Tip   To temporarily hide (disable) the entire layer mask, SHIFT-click the layer mask thumbnail in the Layers panel. SHIFT-click it again to enable the layer mask again. You can also view the layer mask only by ALT-(Windows)/OPTION-(Mac) clicking it.

FIGURE 8-16 Layer masks allow you to combine the best parts of multiple images.

9

Advanced Image "Doctoring"

How to...

- Clone pixels
- Heal textures after cloning
- Use several different healing tools
- Remove red eyes from photos
- Create realistic fakes
- Use reference material

In this chapter, we get to dig into image "doctoring," which in effect means creating a visual forgery. Using the techniques we'll cover in this chapter, we can put ourselves on the moon, or in a jar, or we can remove people (or other objects) from photos. These features of Photoshop are so widely known that pop culture has created a new verb around it, such as "I'm going to Photoshop you out of my wedding pictures because I don't love you anymore," or "I can't accept these photos as evidence in this case because they've obviously been Photoshopped."

Before we get into this, let me put on my grumpy old man hat and just say that any image adjustments that create a new reality should be used for artistic or entertainment purposes only. Every so often, some jerk will create a doctored image of the Loch Ness Monster, or worse, the September 11 terrorist attacks in New York City. Their intention, perhaps, is to feel powerful because they stir up controversy with the power of their Photoshop skills. Don't be that guy. Okay, grumpy old man hat removed; let's start bending reality.

Cloning

The real core of image doctoring resides with an old, but handy tool, the Clone Stamp tool. The Clone Stamp tool simply copies and pastes portions of an image. Because of this, we can copy and paste things into areas where they don't exist. We can also copy background pixels over other pixels, let's say someone's legs, to give the illusion that they're floating. Most of the concepts we'll look at in this chapter deal in some way with cloning.

Using the Clone Stamp Tool

Using the Clone Stamp tool is a little counterintuitive at first. Go ahead and select it from the Tools panel. The Clone Stamp tool looks like a little rubber stamp, and you can find it directly underneath the Brush tool.

Figure 9-1 shows my original image: a photograph of my dog, Gallagher. What we're going to do is remove Gallagher from this photo. To do this, we're going to clone the background, and paint it on top of him.

To clone pixels, hold down the ALT (Windows)/OPT (Mac) key, and click somewhere in your image. Your cursor will turn into crosshairs while you hold down the ALT/OPT key. Clicking once will sample (copy) those pixels. Then, when you go to

FIGURE 9-1 A photo of Gallagher the dog

paint with the Clone Stamp tool, you'll be painting with the pixels you just sampled. In this case, I'm going to ALT/OPT-click around the dog to sample those pixels, and then I'll paint on top of the dog with those pixels. You'll also notice while you're painting that your cursor will have a small overlay of the area that you sampled. This serves as a guide to help you align your strokes, and to see what the final results will look like.

Note You only need to hold down the ALT/OPT key while you're clicking to sample the area you want to clone from, not while you're painting with the Clone Stamp tool.

To complete this process, just repeat the process of sampling (copying) pixels and painting (pasting) them. To cover the dog's body area, you'll need to clone the carpet, and paint with the carpet pixels on top of the dog. As seen in Figure 9-2, to cover the area of the dog's head, you'll need to sample pixels from the armoire behind the dog's head.

FIGURE 9-2 After sampling the background and then painting with the Clone Stamp tool on top of the dog

FIGURE 9-3 The final result after continuing to clone and paint over the dog

And so, cloning to remove objects is as simple as repeating this process over and over again. Simple? Yes. But it is also a whole pile of tedious. As with any painting task, there is no way to automate the process. After several minutes of this process, I came up with the result seen in Figure 9-3. The dog is completely removed from the image. Actually, the dog wasn't removed at all, he was simply painted over. Cloning is certainly an art form, and as with any art form, you only get good with practice.

You can also use the Clone Stamp tool to duplicate objects. If you had a photo of a fire, for example, you could sample the flames and paint more of them to create the illusion of a larger fire.

Using the Aligned Option

With the Clone Stamp tool selected, the Options bar at the top of the interface will display an option called Aligned, which is turned on by default. I hate when this option is selected, but everyone else I know loves it. Before we see what it does, we need to back up a little and look a little more closely at the way cloning works.

When you sample an area with the Clone Stamp tool, it remembers the spot you sampled from. While you're clicking to paint, Photoshop will place a plus sign (+) at the spot where you sampled pixels. You'll notice that as you drag while painting with this tool that the plus sign moves as well. This is because the clone source point also moves while you paint. This is helpful when you're cloning a larger or more complex object, such as a person. You can ALT/OPT-click to sample from their torso, for example, and then continue to paint their entire body without having to resample.

With the Aligned option selected, you don't have to drag in order for the clone source point (the place where you sampled) to copy your movements. If you click once to paint the sampled pixels, and then, say, move your cursor 20 pixels to the right, the area that you sampled will also move 20 pixels to the right.

If the Aligned option is turned off, then as long as you don't drag while painting with the Clone Stamp tool, the clone source point will stay in the same place. Let's say that you wanted to clone out clouds from an otherwise blue sky. Perhaps there is only a small spot of blue sky showing through, and you want to use this as the source point to clone over all clouds. Having Aligned turned off will allow you to continuously sample from that same point.

Healing

Oftentimes when I'm cloning, especially with patterns, the results begin to look terrible. This is because patterns are often difficult to keep pristine with the Clone Stamp tool. Figure 9-4 shows the end result of a pattern cloning gone horribly wrong, resulting in something I call "clone stamp mush." I tried to clone and paint the grass onto the leaves area, and you can see exactly what I did. In creating visual fakery, you never want to leave breadcrumbs of what you did. It should appear that the image was never taken into Photoshop. This is an intentionally exaggerated example, but you can see how the pattern looks very synthetic and fake.

FIGURE 9-4 "Clone stamp mush"

Enter the healing tools, which are designed to fix the exact problem seen in Figure 9-4. They don't copy and paste entire pixels like the Clone Stamp tool does; they only sample patterns while leaving color and lighting information intact.

The Patch Tool

We're going to begin our look at the healing tools with the Patch tool. The Patch tool is, in my opinion, the most powerful and useful of all healing tools. While other cloning and healing tools require you to use brushes, the Patch tool allows you to use selections. You can use existing selections, or you can create them with the Patch tool, which can function like the Lasso tool. While brushes are very powerful, selections give you much more control for tasks like healing.

In the image from Figure 9-4, I'm going to make a selection with the Patch tool around the clone stamp mush area I created. Then I'll put my cursor inside of the selection and drag the selection to an area that I want to use to replace the texture of the selected area. In this case, I'll drag this selection to the grass area. Notice how this adds the grass texture to the clone stamp mush area (see Figure 9-5).

FIGURE 9-5 The Patch tool
restored texture to the cloned area.

 Caution   The healing tools do not like extreme light and dark values. Often, having those values in your Patch tool selection will create weird smears and other artifacts that obviously don't belong. To fix this, keep those areas out of your selection.

You can also use the healing tools, such as the Patch tool, to place texture where it doesn't belong, to create interesting results. In Figure 9-6, I selected the entire grass area by using the Patch tool and dragged the selection up into the trees in the top of the image. Notice how the result allows the grass to maintain its color and lighting, but the grass texture has been replaced by the texture of the branches above.

The Healing Brush Tool

The Healing Brush tool icon looks like a Band-Aid and is grouped in the Tools panel with the Patch tool. Don't confuse this tool with the Spot Healing Brush tool, which looks like a Band-Aid with a marquee selection.

The Healing Brush tool has the same purpose as the Patch tool, but it functions more like the Clone Stamp tool. You can ALT/OPT-click to sample the texture of an area, and then click to

paint with it. So, use the Patch tool if you like the flexibility of working with selections for this type of task. Use the Healing Brush if you've grown accustomed to the Clone Stamp tool workflow and prefer to work with brushes and sampling.

FIGURE 9-6 After using the Patch tool to replace the grass texture with the branches

The Spot Healing Brush

The Spot Healing Brush tool, grouped with the Patch and Healing Brush tools, attempts to remove blemishes with a single brushstroke. No need for cloning. No need for selections. And it actually works pretty well, except you need to remember my advice earlier in this chapter about avoiding light and dark extremes.

When you paint with this tool, it will look like you are painting with semitransparent black until you release the mouse button. This paint should completely encompass the blemish you are trying to remove. Also, do your best to not get too much of the "paint" stroke from the Spot Healing Brush tool outside of the blemish. Generally speaking, with the painting and cloning tools, it's a good idea to dab instead of to paint with long strokes. You can also check the section at the end of this chapter about getting the best results possible from these tools. Figure 9-7 shows a close-up of some ostrich eggs in the photograph we were looking at earlier in this chapter.

FIGURE 9-7 The ostrich eggs

FIGURE 9-8 The ostrich eggs are removed by painting on them with the Spot Healing Brush tool.

What I'm going to do is select the Spot Healing Brush tool and paint over the eggs. Once I release the mouse, these eggs disappear (see Figure 9-8).

You might try a similar effect with a file of your own and get frustrated that you didn't get the same results. It helps to

Remove "Red-Eye" from Photos

Removing red-eye from photographs is not usually something people think of when the topic of image doctoring comes up. But we'll cover this issue because the Red Eye tool is grouped with all of the other tools we've looked at in this chapter.

The red-eye effect is caused when a camera flash reflects off of the back of the eye, usually in low-light situations. The red reflection creates an eerie red glow on the eyes.

To remove this red-eye effect, simply select the Red Eye tool from the Tools panel and click the red of the eye. The red will be neutralized, and the pupil of the eye will appear normal.

know what's going on behind the scenes with this tool. What the Spot Healing Brush tool is doing is looking for pixels around the blemish, and then replacing the blemish with those pixels. But Photoshop can't recognize grass or trees or leaves as grass or trees or leaves. This is an intelligent tool, but it's not *that* intelligent. This tool is great for things like facial blemishes, but if you were going to use this tool to paint out features on an entire human face, for example, Photoshop would not look for other skin tones to use to cover the facial features. It would instead use whatever pixels happened to be adjacent—perhaps pixels from hair, ears, and so on. So, in this case, Photoshop might attempt to cover the eggs with the tall grass nearby, or the leaves, or the branches. Your results may also vary, depending on how large your Spot Healing Brush stroke is.

The good news is that you can just keep painting until Photoshop accurately guesses which adjacent pixels you'd like to replace the blemish. If Photoshop replaced my eggs with some grass and a rock I didn't want, I wouldn't need to undo. I would just paint over the rock using the Spot Healing Brush.

Creating Realistic Fakes

Finally, in this section, we're going to look at a smattering of tips and concepts to use when doctoring images. Some of the items in this section will be technical, while others will be artistic.

You may not be able to use all of these tricks right now, but you can keep this around as reference for when you need it.

Note the Light Source

Although light source doesn't have much to do with cloning, when you're creating digital fakes, this is huge. Especially when combining elements from multiple sources, you may need to flip objects horizontally (discussed in the next chapter) to make them match the light source in the background. This is one of the quickest ways to spot a digital fake. Newbies never try to make every part of a composite have a unified light source. A unified light source means that all elements appear to be lit by the same light. You can create the illusion of an unified light source with shadow layer styles, image adjustments, and masks.

Use Reference Material

Reference material is crucial for creating realistic elements. "Reference material" refers to images, video, or other materials that you look to for reference. For example, if you were creating an ad that had a famous city as an object in a large aquarium, you would obviously need to fake it with Photoshop. But how would you know what a city looks like underwater? You'd have to find photos of other (ideally similar in material) objects underwater to get the feel for how objects respond to light and refraction and other properties of water submersion. If you find yourself in the position most people are and don't have an entire library of photos of various objects underwater, then do what the pros do—use a Google image search. Just go to www.google.com, click Images, and search the amazing wealth of free images available to you there.

Cloning Tricks

We're now going to look at a few tricks that you can use while cloning to help you achieve a better result. It's amazing how much the following simple helpers can enhance the quality of your doctored images.

Using the Clone Source Panel

The Clone Source panel (found on the Window menu) contains a plethora of extra cloning features.

My favorite feature of this panel is the ability to store multiple clone sources. When we cloned the image of my dog earlier, we cloned the carpet, the armoire, and other elements such as the shadows in order to achieve the final result. If we had selected a separate clone source for each element, we wouldn't have had to constantly resample each one. Think of these sources as a bank where you can store different cloned elements that you can retrieve at any time.

To save to a different clone source, simply click one of the five clone source buttons at the top of the Clone Source panel and ALT/OPT-click with the Clone Stamp tool to sample pixels and create a new clone source. To access that clone source later, just click it in this panel. Note that if you have a clone source selected when you create a new sample, then the old sample will be replaced by the new one. So, for instance, if you clicked the third clone source button and ALT/OPT-clicked on clouds, then you would be painting with clouds. If you clicked on another clone source and sampled something else, your clouds would still be stored in clone source 3. But if you ALT/OPT-clicked on a new source with clone source 3 selected, you would replace the clouds with whatever you sampled.

Cloning on a Separate Layer

By now, you know how much I love layers and why I use them so often. You can use the power of layers when you're cloning, and I heartily recommend it. Imagine how much you can destroy an image with cloning!

However, when you create a new layer and try to clone on that, nothing happens when you paint. This is because the default settings only sample the current layer. So if you create a new blank layer, then Photoshop is only sampling the current blank layer. In effect, you're sampling and painting nothing.

What you have to do to get this to work is to change the Sample drop-down in the Options bar from Current Layer to All Layers. Then, when you sample, you'll be sampling from the composite of all layers. And when you paint, you'll be painting on the blank layer. The great purpose of this is that you can remove the cloned pixels at any time. You can also take advantage of any other features of layers: you can select the cloned pixels, duplicate them, lower their opacity, blend them into the original using blend modes, color adjust them independently, and much more.

Zoom In

Perhaps the quickest tip of all here is to zoom in closely while you're cloning. Sometimes, image doctoring (especially cloning) can look all right from far away, only to shock and horrify when seen up close. Zoom in closely while cloning, and the results will be much better when you zoom back out.

Opacity and Soft Edges

You can use the Opacity setting in the Options bar to reduce the opacity of your clone strokes. Whenever I'm doing a very important image-doctoring job, I'll take the Opacity value down to about 15%. That way, my cloning will be very subtle. It takes a little longer, but the results are always much better.

In addition to changing the opacity of the paint strokes, you can also decrease the hardness of a brush to feather the edges. When cloning is done with a hard-edged brush, the paint strokes are usually blatant and obvious. Using a soft-edged brush helps the cloned pixels to blend in better with the background they are being painted onto.

Sample Often

Finally, my last tip is to sample often. Especially when using cloning to cover up or remove a large object from an image, it's important to take samples often. Let's talk about the photo of Gallagher again. We used the carpet to clone over the dog. In most images, the carpet would get gradually darker or lighter in different parts of the image. Thus, cloning from the same spot would result in inconsistencies in luminance in the carpet. Sampling often from the area immediately next to the area you're cloning will result in the cloned area more closely resembling the original area in brightness. This will result in a better final product and will aid in further stumping your audience as to how you were able to make pixels do impossible things.

10
Transforms and Smart Objects

How to...

- ■ Move, scale, and rotate objects
- ■ Flip objects horizontally or vertically
- ■ Use the new Content-Aware Scale feature
- ■ Warp and distort objects
- ■ Avoid damaging objects when transforming

In this chapter, we'll look at how to manipulate, or "transform," objects through scaling, rotating, warping, and more. This is all great fun. The downside is that most transformations reduce the quality of an image. Imagine photographing an original painting by Leonardo da Vinci. The photograph wouldn't quite capture all of the quality and nuances of the original painting. Then imagine photocopying your photo. The quality of the image would be reduced even further. Transforming images is like making poor copies of them; every time you do, the quality of the image lessens.

Because of this quality loss, Photoshop has created *Smart Objects,* which allow you to transform objects without degrading image quality. We'll discuss them later in the chapter. Let's begin by looking at how you can transform objects.

Transforming Objects

The world of transforming objects includes moving, flipping, free transforming, scaling, rotating, skewing, and warping them. We'll also look at a brand-new way to intelligently resize images called *content-aware scaling.* You'll be able to do a lot with images after reading this section.

You'll find that transforming comes in handy for all sorts of uses, but it is especially helpful in compositing.

Moving

Moving objects is one of the tasks that you'll probably perform most often in Photoshop, so it's worth taking the time to learn some tricks in this department.

Let's say I have an image like the one in Figure 10-1. Every element is on its own separate layer. That's a whole bunch of layers. Suppose I want to move the vertical wings. I could scroll through the hundreds of layers I might have in this document to find this layer. Or, I could simply select the Move tool in the Tools panel and enable the Auto-Select option in the Options bar. This causes Photoshop to automatically select whatever layer I click. Then I don't have to go searching for this layer in the Layers panel, which is especially great if I was really lax about naming my layers.

FIGURE 10-1 When you're working with a complicated project like this one, the Auto-Select feature of the Move tool can help you select a layer.

Auto-Select is a great feature, but I hardly ever enable it, because it's easy to mistakenly select and move layers. Maybe I'm just all thumbs when it comes to using a mouse, but I found that this feature often caused more harm than good because of all the layers I fiddled with accidentally.

But you can use the following shortcut to have the best of both worlds. With the Move tool selected and the Auto-Select option disabled, hold down the CTRL (Windows)/CMD (Mac) key while clicking to auto-select a layer. Using this trick, you only select layers when you intend to. This is the way I prefer to work, but you may prefer to always use Auto-Select, or to never use it.

You can also right-click with the Move tool while your cursor hovers over the layer you want to select. A list of layers underneath your cursor will pop up, and you can choose the layer from the list to select the layer.

Flipping

Flipping is when you flip layers, either horizontally or vertically. Figure 10-2 shows our original image.

FIGURE **10-2** The original image

If we wanted to put the girl on the left and the boy on the right, we could do so quickly by flipping the layer horizontally. We can do that by going to the Edit menu with the layer selected and choosing Transform | Flip Horizontal. This mirrors the layer so that we're seeing the reverse (see Figure 10-3).

If you try to flip (or perform most other transforms with) a background layer, the transform options in the Edit menu will be gray and unavailable. You must first unlock the background layer by double-clicking it and then clicking OK in order to select and then flip it.

FIGURE **10-3** After flipping the layer horizontally

Now, I'll undo this action by using CTRL-Z (Windows)/CMD-Z (Mac). I want to flip it again, but this time I'll flip it vertically. This will make it look like the kids are hanging from the ceiling (see Figure 10-4). To do this, choose Edit | Transform | Flip Vertical.

FIGURE **10-4** The result of flipping the layer vertically

From my experience, flipping layers horizontally is useful far more often. I use it when I might want to change the fundamental composition of my image. I might want someone to be facing a different direction, or I might want the lines and structures in the image to be pointing the other way.

Free Transforming

Free Transform is a way to transform an object in many ways at once. When using Free Transform, we enter a mode and in that mode we can scale objects, rotate them, and much more. Let's begin by looking at how to get into Free Transform mode, as well as examining a few concepts that are common to all types of transforms.

To enter Free Transform mode, select a layer and choose Edit | Free Transform. Because Free Transform is something that you will probably do quite often, it pays to remember the keyboard shortcut for it, which is CTRL-T (Windows)/CMD-T (Mac).

Tip When you have some tools selected (such as the selection tools), you can access Free Transform by right-clicking and selecting Free Transform from the context menu.

FIGURE **10-5** The bounding box that surrounds layers in Free Transform mode

When you've entered Free Transform mode, your object will have a rectangular outline around it called a *bounding box,* as shown in Figure 10-5. We'll use the nodes (squares) on this bounding box to make many of our adjustments in this chapter.

It is extremely important to note that you are prohibited from doing any other work in Photoshop until you either accept or cancel the changes you've made in Free Transform mode. You're not allowed to just rotate and run. If you try to make a change in Free Transform mode and then do something else, like select a different tool in the Tools panel, you will get a pop-up asking what you want to do with the changes you've made. Clicking the Apply button will apply the changes and exit Free Transform mode. Clicking Cancel will close the pop-up and allow you to continue working in Free Transform mode. Clicking Don't Apply will exit Free Transform mode and disregard all changes you've made. You can also apply the changes by pressing ENTER on the numeric keypad, or disregard all changes by pressing ESC. Or, you can go to the right side of the Options bar and click the checkmark icon, as shown in Figure 10-6, to accept, or you can click the universal "no" sign (circle with a slash through it) to exit without applying changes.

FIGURE **10-6** Click the checkmark to accept changes you've made in Free Transform mode, or click the circle with a slash through it to exit without making changes.

Tip   If you make a mistake while in Free Transform mode, just use the keyboard shortcut CTRL-Z (Windows)/CMD-Z (Mac) to undo it.

You can also enter Free Transform mode when using the Move tool by selecting the Show Transform Controls option in the Options bar. This will show you a layer's bounding box when it is selected. You can then adjust one of the nodes on the edges or corners of the bounding box as we'll see momentarily, and that will automatically put you in Free Transform mode.

Scaling

Scaling means making something larger (scaling up) or smaller (scaling down). To scale a layer, enter Free Transform mode. If you grab and move one of the nodes (or "handles" as Photoshop calls them) in the center of the left or right edge of the bounding box, you will scale the layer horizontally. Notice how the layer gets disproportionately squished (see Figure 10-7). When I meet people over the Internet, I usually horizontally scale pictures of myself before sending them so I look thinner.

FIGURE 10-7   After scaling down the text horizontally

The Dangers of Free Transform

Every time you use Free Transform to alter the pixels in an object, you degrade the quality of the image a little. And if you use Free Transform to increase the layer size at all, it degrades the object even more. The moral of the story: Use Free Transform sparingly.

Therefore, apply all of your transforms (such as skew, scale, and so on) in one transform session. That will avoid the image degradation that will occur when using Free Transform more than once. To do this in one transform session, you might need to do some planning, but your final image will be all the better for it.

Later in this chapter, we'll look at Smart Objects, which will allow you to use Free Transform as often as you want without any loss in quality.

FIGURE **10-8** After scaling up the text vertically

You can also grab one of the handles in the center of the top or bottom edges of the bounding box to scale the layer vertically (see Figure 10-8). This is great when you want to squash down a layer.

You can also drag on the corner handles to resize a layer in both directions at once. After playing with layer scaling for a while, you might notice that there's too much freedom here. It's all too easy to make your layer smashed or stretched in one way or another. What if you just want to proportionately shrink a layer? Simply hold SHIFT while scaling to keep the width and height of the object in proportion to each other.

 Scaling can quickly destroy the quality of an image. Scaling up a layer made of pixels is always a huge no-no. Also, once you've scaled down a layer (reduced its size), you can't scale it back to its original size without losing quality. Be careful and plan ahead!

You might have noticed that objects scale out from the side of the bounding box opposite the handle you chose to make your transformation. So, if you click on the upper-right corner to shrink the layer, it would scale from the lower-left corner.

If that behavior isn't what you're looking for, you can also hold down the ALT (Windows)/OPTION (Mac) key while scaling from the center of the bounding box. Using this keyboard shortcut, as well as pressing SHIFT to constrain proportions, only toggles this behavior. As soon as you let go of the keys on your keyboard, the behavior will go back to its default. Thus, let go of the mouse first, and then release the keyboard shortcuts.

You can also select part of a layer to transform. In Figure 10-9, I've selected only the *r* in "rock" by using the Lasso tool, and then entered Free Transform mode. Even though the rock text is only one layer, I can still adjust pieces of it independently by using selections and Free Transform mode.

FIGURE **10-9** Pieces of layers can be adjusted by using selections in conjunction with Free Transform mode.

You can also move parts of a layer independently from the rest of the layer by selecting them and then moving them with the Move tool.

Content-Aware Scaling Content-aware scaling is a new feature in Photoshop CS4 that does just what it says: it is aware of the content of a layer when it scales. It's just so intelligent that it creeps me out a little. Figure 10-10 shows my original image—a photo of trees that we looked at earlier in this book.

FIGURE 10-10 The original image of the trees

Now, before we get into content-aware scaling, let's just see what this image would look like if we horizontally scaled it with Free Transform. I'll enter Free Transform mode, and then drag the handle on the right edge of the bounding box to the left, to about the halfway mark. Notice how squashed and unnatural the trees look now (Figure 10-11).

Next, we'll do the same thing, but instead of doing it with Free Transform, we'll choose Edit | Content-Aware Scale. Now, when we scale, Photoshop is aware of the content of the photo and attempts to scale the background while leaving the subject (the trees) as untouched as possible. Notice how natural the final product looks in Figure 10-12. Compare this to Figure 10-10 to see that Photoshop mostly just scaled the background.

This feature is useful when you want to crop an image, but don't want to cut any of the features of the image. This also

FIGURE 10-11 The trees image after scaling the image with Free Transform

allows you more flexibility when you're creating a composition because you can take the "perfect" photo and change the proportion of the image without changing its content.

Rotating

FIGURE 10-12 After you scale the trees with Content-Aware Scale, the trees maintain most of their original proportion.

To rotate an object, enter Free Transform mode, and put your cursor slightly outside of the bounding box near one of the

corner handles. Your cursor will turn into a curved, double-headed arrow. With that icon visible, drag left/right or up/down to rotate the object.

Skewing and Distorting

In Photoshop terms, skewing is like italics for objects, giving them a slant to one side or another. In this section, we'll look at skewing objects, but we'll also look at the other "hidden" transforms as well. If you right-click an object when in Free Transform mode, you get a list of all the available transforms (see Figure 10-13).

First choose Skew. To use the Skew transform, click one of the handles on the sides of the bounding box. When Skew is selected, you will get a double-headed arrow when your mouse hovers over one of these points. Drag to skew the object. Skew is good for when you want an object to look like it's windblown or otherwise being pulled in a certain direction (see Figure 10-14).

FIGURE 10-13 Right-clicking on an object in Free Transform mode yields a menu that shows what's possible in Free Transform mode.

Next, let's look at the Distort transform. Right-click in the Free Transform bounding box and choose Distort. Other than the "biggies" (Scale and Rotate), this is the transform that I probably use the most. Distort allows you to distort an object as if it were in 3D. Grab one of the corner handles and move it toward the center. The pixels in the object not only move, but also scale to create the illusion of 3D movement (see Figure 10-15).

FIGURE 10-14 The logo after skewing

Another variation on distorting is Perspective. This transform creates the illusion that an object is sinking back into 3D space, like the opening credits on *Star Wars* movies. As before, right-click an object in Free Transform mode and select Perspective. In my example, I just dragged to the left with the upper-right corner handle on the bounding box. Both corners scale toward the center in unison, creating the effect that the top of the text is receding into the background, as shown in Figure 10-16.

FIGURE 10-15 The logo after distorting

FIGURE **10-16** The logo after using the Perspective transform

Shortcuts for Distorting

Sometimes right-clicking to access different types of transforms seems inefficient. If you want to access Skew, Distort, and Perspective with keyboard shortcuts, here's how to do it:

- **Skew**   Hold CTRL-SHIFT (Windows)/CMD-SHIFT (Mac) while dragging one of the edge handles.

- **Distort**   Hold CTRL (Windows)/CMD (Mac) while dragging one of the corner handles.

- **Perspective**   Hold CTRL-ALT-SHIFT (Windows)/CMD-OPTION-SHIFT (Mac) while dragging one of the corner handles.

Warp is another transform, but we'll save the Free Transform Warp for a larger discussion on warping in Chapter 13.

   **Transform Selections**

One of the things that many users of Photoshop don't realize is that you can actually transform selections as well as objects. This is helpful when your selection is a little too small, or not wide enough, or for selecting objects that are rotated a little.

To transform a selection, make a selection and then choose Select | Transform Selection. You'll get a Free Transform bounding box. You can resize, rotate, skew, distort, and much more, but it only affects the selection. As with Free Transform, you must accept or cancel the transform in order to exit the selection transform mode.

Mini-Project

Because Free Transform adjustments can all start to seem too similar after a while, we'll take a creative break here, and look at a mini-project that uses Free Transform. Figure 10-17 shows a photo with a logo over it. The logo was taken from the collection of vector shapes that ships with Photoshop.

FIGURE 10-17 The lake image with the target shape over it

We want this logo to appear to be a real, 3D object that was part of this photo. So the first thing to do is to convert this layer to a Smart Object. Right-click the shape layer in the Layers panel, and select Convert To Smart Object. This will ensure that we won't destroy the original target, and that it won't degrade as we transform it. We'll cover what Smart Objects are a little later in this chapter.

Next, use the Distort transform to make this object appear to be in 3D. Enter Free Transform, right-click the logo, select Distort, and drag the corner handles to create the distortion (see Figure 10-18).

FIGURE 10-18 After using the Distort transform on the logo

When using Free Transform to composite objects (such as the logo in Figure 10-18) into the scene, it sometimes helps to use any straight lines that might be in the photo as a guide to how your bounding box should be distorted.

The next step is to copy the layer, and then to perform a Flip Vertical transformation on the bottom copy. This layer will be used as the object's reflection in the water. Next, use the Distort Transform again (on the copy this time) to make it appear that the copy is the reflection in the water. The closer the reflection is to the original, the closer the logo will appear to the surface of the water. It's also a good idea to make the reflection layer's corner handles that are closest to the logo closer to each other than the corner handles away from the logo are to each other. You can see the effect of this in Figure 10-19.

FIGURE 10-19 Adjusting the copy to be the reflection in the water

Next, we'll add some finishing touches on the reflection. First, put the layer with the reflection into the Overlay blend mode so that it interacts with the water in a more realistic way. I'll also lower the opacity of the layer a little. Next, I'll apply the Color Overlay layer style, and change the color to a slightly darker red. Then, I will go to the Filter menu, and choose Blur | Gaussian Blur. I'll increase the Radius value to blur the logo, which will soften the edges and add more realism. Finally, I will add a layer mask, and paint on the far right edge of the logo to fade out the portion of the reflection farthest from the logo (see Figure 10-20).

FIGURE 10-20 The final result. Thank you, Free Transform!

Using Smart Objects

As we've touched on previously in this book, the secret to successful image editing or graphic design or anything else in Photoshop, is nondestructive editing. A synonym for "destructive" here is "permanent." *Nondestructive editing* means making changes that you can change at any time.

Smart Objects allow many functions of Photoshop such as transforming and filters to become nondestructive. For all intents and purposes, what Smart Objects do is allow you to work on a copy of the original object while maintaining a link to the original object. So, if you scaled down a regular layer, and then sized it back up again, it would look awful because data was thrown away when it was scaled down. But if you did the same thing with a Smart Object, it would look fine because it is constantly getting its information from the original object at the original size.

Creating Smart Objects

You can import objects as Smart Objects (as we'll look at momentarily), or you can convert an existing layer or group of layers into a Smart Object. To create a Smart Object, simply select a single layer, or hold SHIFT while selecting multiple layers. Then right-click one of the layers in the Layers panel, and select Convert To Smart Object. Smart Objects are denoted by a special icon, as shown in this illustration, on their layer thumbnail in the Layers panel.

 You can also group several Smart Objects into another Smart Object!

For the most part, Smart Objects function similarly to the way any other layer works in Photoshop. The most noticeable difference is that Free Transform doesn't degrade the quality of the object, and effects applied as filters (discussed later in Chapter 13) are not permanent.

Tip If you ever want to have a Smart Object become a regular old layer again, you can right-click the layer in the Layers panel and select Rasterize Layer.

Working with Imported Smart Objects

You can place objects into Photoshop, and they will become Smart Objects. To place an object as a Smart Object, select File | Place, then navigate to the file you want to place, select it, and click OK. Using this procedure, you can bring in Illustrator art, and all of the brushes and color and everything else you set up in Illustrator will stay intact in Photoshop. Although art from Adobe Illustrator isn't directly editable in Photoshop, you can resize it as much as you'd like without any loss in image quality when it's placed as a Smart Object.

Editing Smart Objects

One of the greatest advantages of Smart Objects is that you can edit their original contents. To do that, simply right-click a Smart Object layer and choose Edit Contents. Whether it's a Smart Object you created or whether it's art from Adobe Illustrator, you can use this feature to edit the original contents. If you select Edit Contents on a Smart Object placed from Illustrator, Photoshop will launch Illustrator for you and open the Smart Object in Illustrator. Simply save your changes in Illustrator, and you will instantly see the update back in Photoshop, without having to place the file again, or do anything else.

Also, when you import a photo and add it to your document as a layer, and then convert that layer to a Smart Object, Photoshop will still remember the source of that Smart Object layer. If you select Edit Original, it will open the original photo for editing.

Saving Smart Objects

Sometime you may want to reuse a Smart Object you've created. Let's say, for example, that you've created a logo from multiple elements and have created a Smart Object from those layers. You can save the Smart Object for later use by right-clicking the Smart Object layer in the Layers panel, and choosing Export Contents. This will create a PSB file that you can import back into Photoshop at any time.

11

Creating and Adjusting Text

How to…

- Create point text
- Create a text box
- Do basic text editing
- Adjust leading and tracking
- Warp text
- Apply layer styles to text
- Create text along a path

Whether you use Photoshop to do logos, graphic design, page layout, or pretty much anything else, text is likely an integral component. Perhaps because of Adobe's top-dog status in the printing world with programs like InDesign and Illustrator, Photoshop has a very powerful arsenal of text-related features. Also, text in Photoshop is vector based, which means that you can increase its size without any loss in quality. In this chapter, we'll look at how to create text and how to format it, distort it, and add effects to it.

Text Creates a New Layer

A valuable aspect of text in Photoshop is that the text exists on its own layer. As soon as you accept your newly created text, Photoshop creates a new text layer for it. The layer thumbnail is a *T*, indicating that this is a text layer, and actual text on the layer becomes the name of the layer.

Having text exist as an independent layer gives you access to the powerful features of layers. You can rearrange the stacking order of text layers. You can CTRL-click (Windows)/CMD-click (Mac) the layer thumbnail to create a selection area in the shape of the text. You can create a layer mask on text layers to mask out portions of the text. You can do all this and much more because text exists as its own layer.

Creating Text

To create text (also called *type* in Photoshop), we usually use the Horizontal Type tool. But we have two ways to create text with this tool, and each yields very different results. Once you've created text—using either method—typing text works similarly to what you would find in any other text editing program, such as Microsoft Word. You can even press ENTER (Windows)/RETURN (Mac) on your keyboard to start a new line of text or a new paragraph.

 You can also create text with the Vertical Type tool, which allows you to create vertically oriented text. This is great for book spines and other narrow spots. But for this chapter, we'll stick to creating the far more common horizontal orientation for text.

Creating Point Text

The quickest and easiest way to create text is to create point text. You create point text simply by clicking with the Horizontal Type tool in a document. Just click once and start typing your text. This can be helpful if you're creating text to go across the bottom line of a poster, or if you're exporting a long string of text for video, such as for a news ticker.

Creating a Text Box

The other way to create text is to drag with the type tool, as you would when creating a marquee with one of the marquee selection tools. This creates a text box. As you type text inside a text box, the text will automatically jump to the next line when it comes to the edge of the text box. A text box tells Photoshop "no matter what happens, don't let text get outside this box." Even if you decide later to resize the text box, the text will still conform to the new confines of the box. Allow me to demonstrate. Figure 11-1 shows a text box I've created with the Horizontal Type tool.

FIGURE **11-1** Text in a text box

Now, I'll resize the text box. Note how the text adjusts itself so that it still fits the box (see Figure 11-2).

With one of the type tools selected, you can hold down the CTRL (Windows)/CMD (Mac) key to temporarily toggle the Move tool. This way, you can move your text into place, release the key, and then continue editing the text.

FIGURE 11-2 After you resize the text box, Photoshop automatically resizes the text to stay within the box.

Formatting Text

Now that we know how to create text, it's time to learn how to format it. The term *format* is a general term that means to adjust the appearance of text. Before we edit it, however, we'll need to learn the rules for selecting text. For simple text adjustments, you can just use the Options bar at the top of the interface. For more advanced text formatting, you'll need to use the Character and Paragraph panels.

Selecting Text to Edit

After creating and accepting your text, you'll start to notice some changes in your cursor. While you have one of the type tools selected, if you put your cursor in an area where there isn't any text, your cursor will look like a text input cursor with a selection marquee-type box around it. This indicates that clicking will create a new text layer.

However, when you place your cursor on top of—or even close to—existing text, that selection marquee-type box will disappear, and the text input cursor will show by itself. This indicates that clicking will adjust text that has already been created. Clicking once would activate text editing mode, which would then allow you to drag to select individual letters, words, or lines of text to edit. As in a text editing "mode" like Free Transform, you'll need to accept or cancel all changes before working in other parts of Photoshop.

Tip   You can also enter text editing mode, and select all the text on that layer at once by double-clicking the text layer's thumbnail in the Layers panel.

Adjusting a Text Box

You can adjust a text box by clicking once in the text box with one of the type tools. Then the nodes on the text box appear. You can drag those to adjust them, as you would the nodes on a Free Transform bounding box. Text inside the text box will automatically adjust to fit the new box size.

Making Simple Text Adjustments

Now, we'll look at how to make basic adjustments to text. For this you'll not only have to be in text editing mode, but you'll also need to drag to select some letters or text to edit. Just entering text editing mode won't make any of the formatting changes we'll address in this section.

The Options bar at the top of the interface groups the most commonly used text editing features in a real handy spot. To see the text options in the Options bar, you'll need to have one of the text tools selected. As we cover the options here, you can use Figure 11-3 as a reference.

FIGURE **11-3** When a text tool is selected, the Options bar gives you the most-used text options.

From left to right, the third option we come to is the font drop-down (which is currently displaying Poplar Std, in this case). When you click this drop-down, Photoshop shows you a list of available fonts and a preview of each font (see Figure 11-4). You can also click once in the text area of the font drop-down, and then use the arrow keys to browse through different fonts.

 To simultaneously change the font of all of the text on a layer, select the text layer in the Layers panel (without going into text editing mode), and then change the font.

The next drop-down is the font style. Not all fonts will have font styles available. Font styles are typically things like bold, italics, light, and other font variations. I'll show you how to fake many of those options later in this chapter.

To the right of font style is another important text option: font size. To input a font size, you can click the arrow icon to open the drop-down, and then select one of the preset sizes. You can also drag to highlight the current font size value, and then type a new value. But my favorite way to increase text size is actually somewhat hidden. Hover your mouse directly on the $_TT$ icon for text size in the Options bar. Your cursor will turn into a finger with a double-headed arrow. When you see this icon, drag to the left to scale down your text, and drag to the right to increase the size of your text. Aside from being a quick way to increase or decrease text size, this method offers another added benefit: you can watch your text scale up and down as you change this value. That way, you don't have to guess how large you want your text to be.

The next option is anti-aliasing. This is a more advanced option that essentially controls the crispness of the edges of your text. Unless you're creating very small text for web pages (in which case you may want to turn off anti-aliasing to make the text more legible), it's probably best to leave this setting alone.

FIGURE 11-4 The font drop-down list. Notice the sample of each font on the right side of the drop-down.

We then have the three most common alignment options—left align, center align, and right align. These options determine the justification of your paragraph.

Immediately to the right of the alignment options is a little rectangle. This is actually a color swatch. To change the color of the currently selected text, click the color swatch to open the Color Picker, and choose a new color. You can also move your cursor outside of the Color Picker dialog box to sample colors from your document. In the example seen in the first few figures of this chapter, I sampled the blue from the sky to get the color of the text. This can create a more cohesive feel in a graphic layout.

Finally, the Options bar has two icons—one for opening up warp options, and the other for opening the Character and Paragraph panels.

Intermediate Text Formatting

While the text options in the Options bar are all you might need in many situations, you'll often find yourself wanting more control. What if you want more space between lines of text? Or what if you want to adjust the spacing between text characters? The Character and Paragraph panels are where we go to make much more advanced formatting changes to your text. For the remainder of this section, we'll be looking specifically at the Character panel.

The Character Panel

With a type tool selected, open the Character panel by clicking the button on the right end of the Options bar. At first, the Character panel, shown in Figure 11-5, might seem a little intimidating with all of its hieroglyphic-like icons. The good news is that you can take advantage of this helpful panel without knowing what all these features do.

FIGURE **11-5** The Character panel

Leading   We see in the Character panel many of the same features we also saw in the Options bar. One of the most useful features of the Character panel is the ability to adjust leading (pronounced "ledding," not "leeding"). Leading is the space between lines of text. It comes from the olden days of printing presses when pieces of lead were stuck in between lines of type to space them out. The leading icon can be found in the upper-right corner of the Character panel, and it looks like two stacked *A*'s. Figure 11-6 shows what my text from earlier in this chapter looks like with the leading value decreased.

FIGURE **11-6** The text with decreased leading

Tracking   While leading is the space between lines of text, tracking is the space between all characters on a line. In the Character panel, you'll find the tracking value below the leading value, and the tracking icon looks like *AV* over a double-headed arrow. As we increase this value, the characters spread out more (see Figure 11-7).

FIGURE **11-7** The text with increased tracking

The Style Buttons   Earlier in this chapter, we talked a bit about font styles, such as bold, italics, and so forth. A row of buttons at the bottom of the Character panel (see Figure 11-5) allows you to create such styles if you don't have a font that contains them. While this is a nice feature, it's often better to use fonts with these styles built in, if possible. Most of these styles use the term *faux,* which means artificial. You'll probably get better results from a bold font than from a regular font with an artificial bold style applied. The following table lists what these eight buttons, from left to right, do. Keep in mind that in most cases, these styles are not mutually exclusive. For example, you can apply both faux bold and faux italics to the same text.

Faux Bold	This is a fake bold style, which makes text thicker, like **this**.
Faux Italic	This is a fake italics, which gives a slight slant to the text. This is typically used for emphasis, like *this*.
All Caps	This makes every letter a capital letter. IT'S REALLY GOOD FOR TEXT THAT IS VERY SERIOUS, OR VERY ANGRY. DON'T YOU FEEL INTIMIDATED?
Small Caps	This is like All Caps, but it makes every letter a small capital. However, the letters that you capitalize are larger than the others. Thus, Chad Perkins in the Small Caps style is CHAD PERKINS. This style is often used for professional institutions like banks or law firms because it conveys order and strength.
Superscript	This raises a character from its baseline (the imaginary line on which text sits) and reduces its size. This is good for mathematical powers, such as with 2^{10}, in which *10* has the superscript style applied.
Subscript	This lowers a character below its baseline and reduces its size. This is great for things like chemical formulas. In H_2O, the *2* has the subscript style applied.
Underline	This underlines the text. It is seldom used, except to denote web links, such as www.adobe.com.
Strikethrough	This places a line through text. Typically this is used to cross out text, such as ~~purple spotted buffalo~~.

How to...   Rasterize Text

As I mentioned at the beginning of this chapter, the text we create in Photoshop is vector based, so you can scale text up and down as big and as often as you'd like to without losing any quality.

But sometimes you might not want your text to be text anymore. Let's say that you're going to pass your Photoshop document over to other artists who don't have the fonts that you used. When they open your project, Photoshop might replace the font you used with one of theirs. That could alter your design.

(continued)

Also, you may want to add effects such as a blur to your text. These types of effects (discussed in Chapter 13) are unavailable for text layers. So what are you to do?

The answer is that you must rasterize your text. *Rasterizing* an object means converting it into pixels. It will still appear as text to you, but Photoshop will no longer see it as text, only pixels. To convert a text layer to pixels, simply right-click on a text layer in the Layers panel, and select Rasterize Type.

Often, when I convert text to pixels, I am reminded of the movie, *Superman II*. In that movie, Superman becomes a mortal man so that he could experience a regular life. This is kind of like converting our super powerful text into regular old pixels. For Superman, as it turned out, having the ability to fly, as well as to throw people really far and shoot lasers out of your face isn't so bad after all. So, he went back to being Superman. If you want to apply effects to your text but don't want to downgrade it to mere pixels, right-click a text layer and choose Convert To Smart Object. Although this will take away the ability to directly edit your text (without opening the Smart Object by double-clicking it), this will allow you to edit your text nondestructively.

Warping Text

Photoshop includes some warp styles that allow you to warp your text nondestructively. These warp styles are mostly cheesy and overused. But when used with tact and restraint, they can add some life to your text.

To access the available warp styles, select a type tool, and then click the Create Warped Text button in the Options bar.

After you click the button, the Warp Text dialog box will pop up. You will be unable to adjust any options or to see any changes until you change the Style type from the drop-down at the top of the dialog box (see Figure 11-8). I'll choose the Arc style.

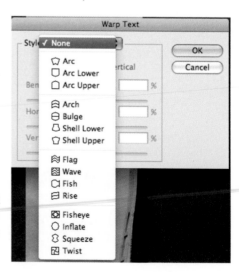

FIGURE 11-8 The Style drop-down in the Warp Text dialog box

At first, the warp effect is a little overstated (see Figure 11-9). Don't worry about that. The default settings are a little over the top, so we'll tone that down.

The Bend value controls the intensity of the warping. The default value is 50, which is rather high. After toning down this value to about 17 and repositioning my text, I get a more appropriate effect (see Figure 11-10). You can also take the Bend value to a negative number, creating a bend in the opposite direction (like a valley instead of a hill).

FIGURE **11-9** The Arc style of warp

FIGURE **11-10** Warped text with the Arc style and a Bend value of 17

You can also adjust the Horizontal and Vertical Distortion sliders to create a pinch effect. In Figure 11-11, I've taken the Horizontal Distortion value to –25.

One of the best features of these warp styles is that they are nondestructive. After you click OK to accept your text, the thumbnail icon for the text layer in the Layers panel will convert to a warped text icon. This shows that Photoshop remembers that this is warped text. That's a good sign. Click the Create Warped Text button in the Options bar again to reopen the Warp Text dialog box and see all of your settings exactly the way you left them. You can alter any settings here, or change the Style back to None to completely remove all warping.

Text and Layer Styles

We've already covered layer styles in this book, so there's no need to revisit the issue in-depth here. But realize that layer styles can be applied to almost any type of layer, including text layers. Figure 11-12 shows my final poster headline. I added a layer style that consists of a Drop Shadow effect, Bevel and Emboss, and Color Overlay.

Now, let's look at one last effect you can apply to your text.

FIGURE 11-11 Warped text with the Arc style, a Bend value of 17, and a Horizontal Distortion value of –25

FIGURE 11-12 My final text, with formatting, warping, and layer styles

Text on a Path

Suppose you want to create text that moves along a *path,* which is what vector shapes in Photoshop are called. Perhaps you wish this text on a path to wrap around a circle or to look like it is waving in the wind. You first need to create a path for the text to follow.

We've already covered how to create shapes that are filled with color. But what about those times when you just want to create a path to be used for text, and you don't want a shape? For those instances, you'll need to change how the shape is created.

Select a shape tool in the Tools panel, and change the option in the Options bar from Shape layers to Paths. This will cause the shape you create to show up as a path in the Paths panel, instead of as a layer in the Layers panel. The path will not be filled with color and will not be visible in any way. This is perfect for what we want for text on a path.

Paths option

Once you've created your path, select one of the type tools, and then click the path with it. Once you start typing, the text will wrap around the shape, as shown in Figure 11-13.

FIGURE **11-13** Text on a path

You'll quickly notice that paths look ugly. You can deselect
paths, making them invisible, by going to the Paths panel and
clicking the path to deactivate it (see Figure 11-14). You can
also deselect the path by simply selecting another layer.

FIGURE 11-14 The final text on
a path, with the path deselected

You can manipulate both the path and the text on the path by using the Select and Direct
Selection tools.

12

Intro to Photoshop Extended

How to

- Import 3D objects
- Choose a 3D application to use
- Create 3D objects in Photoshop
- Manipulate and paint on 3D objects
- Import and export video
- Create animation

Beginning with its previous version (CS3), Photoshop has offered two different versions: the standard version of Photoshop, and another version called Photoshop Extended. At this writing, Photoshop Extended costs about $300 more than the standard version when purchased separately and comes as part of any of the Premium editions of the Creative Suite (for example, Design Premium, Web Premium, and Production Premium). Photoshop Extended includes all of the features of the regular version of Photoshop and adds features for specific industries such as engineering, medicine, 3D, and video.

In this chapter, we'll briefly stroll through some of the key features of Photoshop Extended. We'll focus exclusively on the features that pertain to 3D and video. The improvements made in the current version are quite impressive, to say the least, so this should be educational.

 You can instantly tell if you're using Photoshop Extended because you will have an Analysis menu and a 3D menu at the top of the interface.

3D in Photoshop CS4 Extended

Most 3D objects are created in dedicated 3D programs. The problem is that learning 3D software isn't quite as easy as learning applications like Photoshop. It may take years using 3D software before you can create something that looks believable and lifelike. Photoshop CS4 Extended can be used in lieu of a 3D application because it can create 3D objects. But before we get into making 3D objects, we need to look at the anatomy of a 3D object.

The Anatomy of a 3D Scene

The foundation of a 3D object is a model, also called a *mesh*. Models usually consist of many connected, flat, 2D polygons. Figure 12-1 shows a 3D model imported into Photoshop and put into a wireframe display mode so that we can see its polygons. This model appears here courtesy of Kymnbel Bywater of spilledinkanimation.com.

When I put this back into its default display mode, you can see what these polygons look like when covered with a surface (see Figure 12-2).

The surfaces that we use to "clothe" 3D mesh objects are called *materials*. They are also often referred to as "textures" or "shaders." Materials can be just about any type of image, sometimes even a movie! Let's say a 3D character that you create carries an orb filled with swirling gasses. You could simply create a sphere and cover it in a video texture of swirling gasses.

After creating the 3D mesh object and then covering it in a texture, we typically add lights and cameras. The real secret to creating realistic 3D objects is in the lights. You can make a terrible modeling job look much better—or even good—by using lights well. Figure 12-3 shows our subway scene covered in some lights. The effect is subtle, but our scene is now starting to look a little more realistic.

FIGURE 12-1 In wireframe display, you can see the polyg that make up this 3D object.

FIGURE 12-2 The polygons (the model) covered with a surface

FIGURE **12-3** The subway scene after adding some lighting

We can then add animation to our scene. Finally, when we're all done, we need to output the 3D file, or in other words, *render* it. Rendering might be a new concept for those who have their roots in the print world. In Photoshop, you just save the file and you're done. In the 3D world, rendering is a huge process that can take days. And the way you render the file may make the difference between a horrible final project, and an amazing one. Figure 12-4 shows our final subway scene after using a more advanced system of rendering in Photoshop CS4 called *Ray Traced*, which allows for shadows and reflections.

Opening 3D Files

Photoshop Extended allows you to open 3D files in certain formats, the same way you would open any other type of file. The supported 3D import formats are 3DS, Collada (DAE), KMZ (the 3D format in Google Earth 4), U3D, and OBJ. Once imported, these 3D files behave just as do the files we'll create and paint on next.

FIGURE **12-4** The final subway scene, including models, materials, lights, and enhanced render settings

Which 3D Program You Should Learn

If I had a penny for every time someone asked which 3D program to learn, I'd have at least a couple of bucks. Asking what type of 3D program you should learn (or what type of camera you should purchase) is a little like asking someone what type of car you should drive or what you should name your children. This is something that you should decide for yourself based on your needs and preferences. Thus, in terms of 3D software, not everyone has the same budget, time to learn, preferences, and eye for and concern about quality.

It is so handy to be able to create objects out of nothing, and 3D applications put that power in your hands. But if you want to take your 3D skills to a level beyond Photoshop Extended, be aware that you'll pay a price. Most 3D applications are extremely time-consuming to learn and also are very expensive. Most cost from $3,000 to $12,000. If price is your biggest concern, you can check out a 3D program called Blender. It's free (and legal)! It's also available for Windows, Mac, Linux, and more. You can find it at www.blender.org. Don't let its price fool you—Blender is a very powerful application that can create 3D objects, animate them, and more.

Perhaps the most popular 3D application is 3DS Max by Autodesk. I find 3DS Max to be the most intuitive of all the major 3D packages, although the learning curve is still quite steep. However, although I love 3DS Max, I love working on the Mac operating system more, and 3DS Max is only available on Windows. So, I must go elsewhere for my 3D needs. 3DS Max is currently the undisputed champion in the world of video game creation.

Maxon's Cinema 4D is quickly becoming a popular choice for 3D artists. You can get it for a fair price (about $3,500, depending on the version you purchase), and it is available for both Windows and Mac platforms. Cinema 4D is also widely used because of its unparalleled integration with Adobe's motion graphics application, After Effects.

Autodesk's Maya is probably the leading software application used in feature films. I find Maya really difficult to get started with, but it is unbelievably powerful. It's not difficult to get great 3D results when using Maya. It is available for both Mac and Windows.

Softimage XSI is another of the big 3D players in the film industry. I find XSI easy to get started with, but difficult to master. It's expensive, and it's available only on Windows and Linux.

Lightwave is the little 3D program that could. It started out as a big underdog, but its user base has increased in recent years. Lightwave is becoming increasingly popular in 3D work for television. I can't stand Lightwave. I find it impossible to figure out and work with. But many people swear by it and prefer it over any other 3D package. It's available for Mac and Windows, and, at less than $1,000, it is the cheapest of all the programs mentioned here (other than Blender, of course).

Strata is another great 3D company that also makes plug-ins for Photoshop Extended. If you'd like to get deeper into the 3D world, but spending dozens of hours (and thousands of dollars) with new 3D software is a little too much, I definitely recommend Strata's plug-ins. They're a great balance between the simplicity of Photoshop Extended and a full-fledged 3D package.

This is not a comprehensive list. But if you're interested in making video games or *Shrek* or something else that requires a dedicated 3D program, this should be enough information to get you started on your journey.

Making 3D Objects

Now that you know what makes up 3D objects, let's create some. First, make a new blank layer in the Layers panel. Then fill that layer with the foreground color. I'll fill my layer with a dull brown. If you'd like to use my color, I'm using R-175, G-150, B-95.

 Remember that you can click the upper-left color swatch at the bottom of the Tools panel to open the Color Picker. And you can use the keyboard shortcut ALT-BACKSPACE (Windows)/OPTION-DELETE (Mac) to fill the selected layer with the foreground color.

FIGURE **12-5** Mmmm… 3D donut…

With this new layer selected, go to the 3D menu, and choose New Shape From Layer | Donut. Photoshop will then use the brown layer you just created as the material for a newly created 3D object! (See Figure 12-5.)

You can also create other shapes from the same menu, such as a sphere, cylinder, cube, hat, wine bottle, and more. As we'll soon see, you can adjust these objects to move them around, and then customize their textures.

 3D layers have a small cube icon on their layer thumbnail in the Layers panel.

Manipulating 3D Objects

As with image editing, "manipulate" in the 3D world essentially just means to adjust something. So, we'll look now at a few ways to manipulate a 3D object.

At the bottom of the Tools panel are two tool slots dedicated to 3D tools. Select the 3D Rotate tool, which looks like an orb with a circular arrow around it. With this tool selected and the 3D layer selected in the Layers panel, you'll see a new gadget called the *3D Axes*. Shown in Figure 12-6, this is the new way to adjust 3D objects in Photoshop. This little tool can be used to move, rotate, and scale 3D objects.

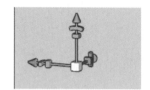

FIGURE 12-6 The 3D Axes

The 3D Axes tool has three arrows: one red, one green, and one blue. Each color corresponds to a different dimension—X, Y, and Z, respectively. At the end of each arrow are three elements: a box, an arc, and an arrow. Dragging the box will scale the object in that direction. You can use this to squash and stretch 3D objects. Dragging the arc will rotate the object in that dimension. And dragging the arrow will move the 3D object in that dimension.

Tip   You can also use the other 3D tools to adjust 3D objects. I just prefer the 3D Axes because it's basically all of those tools in one.

For the time being, I'll leave my 3D donut where it is. Now let's get to painting it.

Painting on 3D Objects

Photoshop CS4 Extended now lets you paint directly onto the surface of a 3D object. This is ideal for creating materials for 3D objects. Let's say that you want to add a pocket to someone's shirt. If you have the shirt material texture open in its own file in Photoshop, how do you know where precisely to put the pocket? That's too much alliteration, and too much guesswork. It's much easier to simply paint the pocket (or whatever else you need) directly on the object.

This process is so easy, I feel guilty even devoting a section of the book to it. Just select the Brush tool (or the Clone Stamp tool), and start painting on the donut! (See Figure 12-7.)

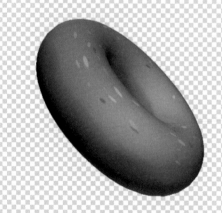

FIGURE 12-7 After painting on the donut

Normally, I would suggest you create a blank new layer and paint on that to be safe. In this case, you'll want to paint directly on the 3D object so that the paint becomes part of the object. That way, when you move the 3D object, the paint goes along with the object because it's part of it. Notice how the paint stays attached to the donut even when the donut is repositioned.

 Tip You can also edit textures directly by double-clicking in the Layers panel on the name of the texture underneath the 3D object it's applied to.

Saving 3D Files

When you want to save your Photoshop 3D work, you have two ways to do it. You can save a regular old Photoshop document (PSD), and your 3D object with all of its materials and lights will be stored in it. You can also select a 3D layer in the Layers panel, and then go to the 3D menu and select Export 3D Layer.

 **How to. . .**

Take Advantage of 3D: The Next Level

We could spend an entire book (and several people have) talking only about the features in Photoshop Extended. We've only scratched the surface in this chapter. If you'd like to further your studies of 3D in Photoshop Extended, I recommend checking out the new 3D panel. The 3D panel is the hub of the new advanced 3D workflow in Photoshop Extended. You can even select the new Advanced 3D workspace from the workspace drop-down in the upper-right corner of the interface. This closes all panels except for the 3D panel and the Layers panel.

At the top of the 3D panel are four buttons. The first one on the left is the Scene filter button. This shows you all of the meshes, materials, and lights in your scene at once. You can also make big changes to your entire scene—such as the render preset you'd like to use—in the Scene filter area. The other three buttons at the top of the 3D panel act as filters. If you have a big scene (3D project), you can click the Meshes button to see just the meshes. Or you can click the Materials button to see just the materials, or the Lights button to see just the lights. In each of these categories, you're given more advanced options for each category. So, if you want to adjust the materials, go to the 3D panel and click the Materials button. You'll not only see just the filters at the top of the panel, but you'll also then get access to further material options at the bottom of the panel.

This allows you to export only the 3D layer for use in other programs. You can save the 3D object in any of the file formats that Photoshop can import (discussed earlier in this chapter), with the exception of 3DS.

Video and Animation in Photoshop CS4 Extended

When video was introduced in Photoshop in Photoshop CS3 Extended, many Photoshop users were scratching their heads, wondering why Photoshop should have video capabilities. For the most part, the only ones who didn't question the move were people who deal with video. They understand that video is nothing more than a series of still images—called *frames*— played back really fast. And, since Photoshop is the emperor of image editing, why not be able to work with video?

The world is becoming increasingly obsessed with having video everywhere. We now have video on cell phones and other mobile devices. Video is becoming all the rage on the Internet. Training through video podcasts is becoming more and more popular. I've even seen refrigerators that have a video screen on the front.

Here, we'll look at some of the basic features for importing, working with, creating, and exporting video. As with 3D, many people have written entire books on using video in Photoshop, so we'll just be taking a quick tour here.

Importing Video

The process by which we import video is identical to the way we import anything else in Photoshop. Choose File | Open, and select a video to import. Once it's imported, you'll want to go the Window menu and open the Animation panel (see Figure 12-8).

 Tip   In the same way that 3D layers are denoted with a cube icon on their layer thumbnail, video layers have a little filmstrip on their layer thumbnails in the Layers panel.

The video formats that are supported include MPEG-1, MPEG-2, MPEG-4, MOV, AVI, and FLV. To avoid most compatibility problems with video, you should have the latest updates of the free Flash Player and the free QuickTime player.

FIGURE 12-8 After importing video with the Animation (Timeline) panel open

Working with Video

Now that we've imported a video clip, let's work with it. The timeline in the Animation panel shows you where in time you are. If you look closely at the timeline, you'll see a thin, red vertical line with a blue top. This is called the Current Time Indicator (CTI). This shows you where in time you are. Dragging the CTI toward the right will fast forward the video. Dragging to

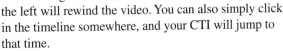

the left will rewind the video. You can also simply click in the timeline somewhere, and your CTI will jump to that time.

To play/pause your video, press SPACEBAR, or press the right-arrow (Play) button in the bottom left corner of the Animation panel.

Tip   You'll notice that video (unlike 3D) has no specific menu. To access most video options, go to the Animation panel fly-out menu.

Creating Animation

You can actually create video and animation from scratch in Photoshop Extended. You might have noticed that all layers in the Layers panel also show up in the Animation panel. This is because most layers can be animated! To see all the properties that can be animated, click the down arrow to the left of the name of the layer in the Layers panel. As shown in Figure 12-9, for most types of layers, you will be able to animate Position, Opacity, and Style (as in layer styles).

To animate all properties, you use the same process. In this example, we'll animate a layer fading in. First, drag your CTI to the beginning of the timeline (all the way to the left). Take the Opacity value for the layer to 0%. Then, click the stopwatch icon next to the word "Opacity" in the Animation panel. This will create a small diamond on the current frame. That small diamond is called a *keyframe*. It remembers values. The diamond is Photoshop's way of telling us that it will be at 0% Opacity at the beginning of the animation. Next, move the CTI to the right just a little. This will determine the point in time at which your video is done fading in. About 2 seconds is a good spot to complete the fade-in. With the CTI at the 2-second mark, take the Opacity value to 100%. Another keyframe is automatically created for you in the Animation panel. And you're done! That's all there is to creating animation in Photoshop.

Photoshop will start at 0% opacity in the beginning and will gradually fade up to 100% opacity over 2 seconds. If you want to make the animation happen over a longer period, simply drag the keyframe on the right (the one that contains the 100% opacity data) farther to the right. If you were to drag the keyframe to the right 1 second, for example, that would be like telling Photoshop that it now has 3 seconds to create the same animation, so it will go more slowly. Likewise, dragging the keyframes closer together will speed up the animation.

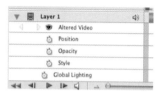

Figure 12-9 After clicking the down arrow next to the names of layers in the Animation panel, we get access to all animatable properties.

Tip   Timecode is a group of numbers separated by colons or semicolons. From left to right, timecode displays *hours; minutes; seconds; frames*. Thus, 0;01;12;07 is 0 hours, 1 minute, 12 seconds, and 7 frames.

Exporting Video

Once you've completed working on your animation or video, you'll need to export it. Exporting video is like rendering 3D files, and as a matter of fact, Photoshop calls it *rendering video*.

You need to render video so that others can view your work. To export your animation or other video work to video, go to File | Export | Render Video. You're then presented with a somewhat gnarly dialog box, as you can see in Figure 12-10. The good news is that you don't need to know what all the options are, just the ones you need.

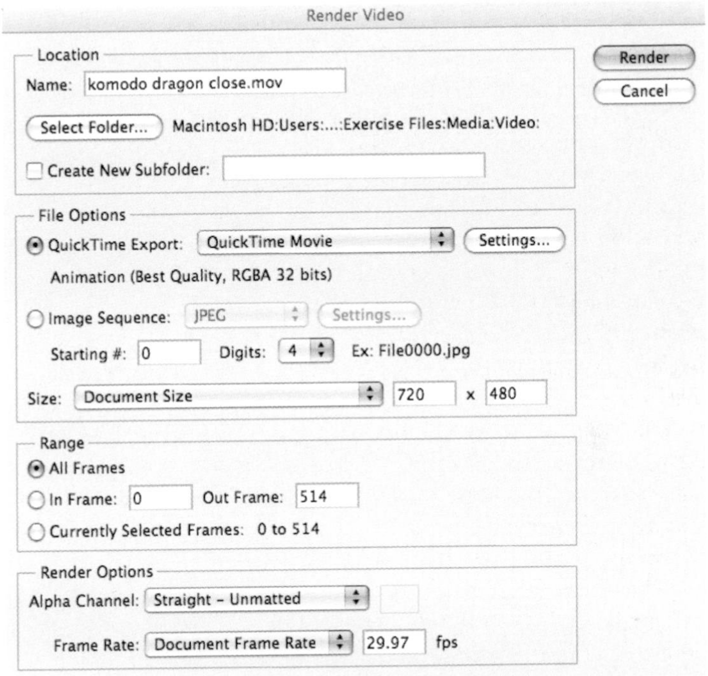

FIGURE 12-10 The Render Video dialog box

We'll cover this from the top down. First things first—name the file, and click the Select Folder button to determine where to save the rendered file. Under the File Options section, you'll see a QuickTime Export drop-down. This doesn't mean that you can export only a QuickTime movie. QuickTime is just the vehicle that Photoshop uses to do its video rendering. In the QuickTime Export drop-down, you'll see some common video file formats, such as QuickTime, AVI (video for Windows), 3G (the standard format for cell phone video), and MPEG-4 (the standard format for podcast video, and video on iPods and iPhones). In the Size drop-down, you can set the final output size. The pixel size of a standard television is 720 pixels (wide) × 480 pixels (tall). The Range option allows you to control how much of your animation you output. Maybe you just want to render a small sample of your 20-minute movie. Range is perfect for that.

When you're done adjusting your settings, click the Render button to start the video exporting process. Be aware that video is not like still images when it comes to output time. When you're dealing with video in Photoshop, you're probably dealing with 30 frames (images) every second. If you have color effects on your video, animated layers, or other changes, output can take a while, so be patient.

 Unlike with 3D files, saving the PSD file that you've imported video into will not save the video file in your PSD. With big files like video, Photoshop (and other video editing programs) only maintains a link to the original file that's on your computer. This means that if you move, rename, or delete the video file, Photoshop will be unable to locate it.

13

Special Effects

How to…

- Apply filters to a layer
- Browse multiple filters using the Filter Gallery
- Use filters nondestructively
- Perform advanced warping with Liquify
- Create organic textures from scratch

Special effects are dear to my heart. Don't get me wrong—I love taking images and making them more beautiful while trying to maintain the illusion that they were just photographed that way. But special effects are a different ball game. You can give someone superhuge eyes, or create water from scratch, or blur out part of an image to draw attention elsewhere. Special effects allow me to invent unnatural scenarios and to let my creativity go crazy. With effects, we're still going for a realistic look—that's very important. If the fire coming out of my nose looks like Photoshop paint, then I've failed. But we are allowed more freedom to delve into the fantastic than we would have with normal photo editing.

Filters

Filters are a large group of effects that we can apply to images. Filters can be anything from blurs to textures to distortions, and everything in between. One thing is common to most filters: they fiddle with the existing pixels of the layer they're applied to.

Filters used to be one of the biggest selling points of Photoshop. Back in the 1990s, in the early days of image editing, it was so cool to be able to add these weird, often psychedelic effects to photos. But after a while, people got tired of the old "check out what my computer can do" type of effects, and they wanted more realism, and for these effects to be used with greater purpose; with a greater sense of design. These days, things have progressed even further, and art has retaken its rightful place as the most important aspect of modern design.

I contend that filters still have a place in modern Photoshop usage; we just have to be more skillful with their implementation. We have to use them with more tact. We have to refine them so they look photorealistic. But that's all part of the fun.

Using Filters

Let's get our hands dirty and see what filters are capable of. I'm starting with the image seen in Figure 13-1. This image appears courtesy of Heather Perkins. It's a great one for demonstrating some sample filters because it has a wide array of textures, from intricate ice to a blurry background. It also has a good tonal balance—bright highlights and darker areas.

FIGURE 13-1 The image we'll be using to demo a smattering of filters

| Note | The terms "effect" and "filter" are often used interchangeably in editing circles. Technically, in the Adobe world, effects are nondestructive filters. Still, effect and filter are essentially synonyms. |

To apply a filter to this image, I'll go to the Filter menu at the top of the Photoshop interface. You might think this menu would have a list of filters, but instead it lists categories of filters, each of which in turn has a long list of filters (see Figure 13-2).

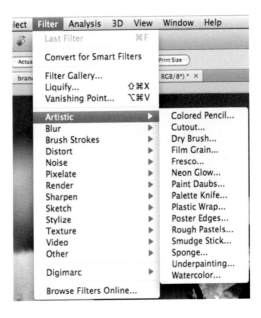

Later in this chapter, we'll look at how to apply filters nondestructively. For now, you may want to apply filters to a duplicate of your original layer, so that the original stays intact.

We'll start at the top and just sprint through this list of filters to get an idea of what is here. Let's go to the Artistic submenu and choose the Cutout filter. With some filters, the filter will just apply to the image at this point. But with many of the more artsy filters (especially those included in the Artistic, Brush Strokes, and Sketch submenus), another window opens called the Filter Gallery, as shown in Figure 13-3.

The Filter Gallery shows you a preview of the effect in the big area on the left of the window. You can also see thumbnails of other effects in the center; you can browse through them if your current result wasn't what you were looking for. To see what your image looks like with another filter, simply click one of the thumbnails. Now that's convenience. On the right

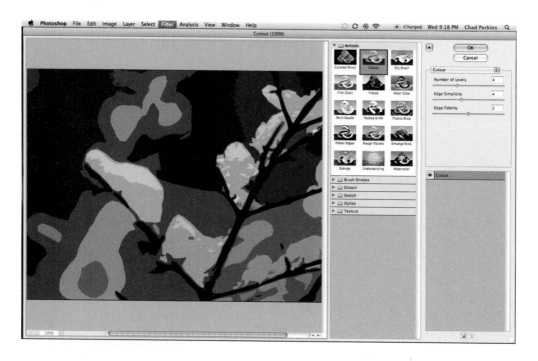

FIGURE 13-3 The Filter Gallery
opens after applying certain effects
like Cutout.

side of the gallery, you can adjust the various parameters of
the currently applied effect. Nothing is actually applied to your
image until you click OK in the Filter Gallery. If you click
Cancel, it cancels everything and your image returns to the way
it was with no filters applied. Speaking of Cancel, I'll click that
to exit the Filter Gallery without saving.

The Filter Gallery is great for those times when you want a "cool effect" on your image, but
you aren't quite sure what that cool effect is. The Filter Gallery specializes in hard-to-describe,
artistic looks that you can apply to images.

Blur Filters

Next, we'll look at the popular blur effects. You'd be amazed at
how often these come in handy. First, I'll choose Filter | Blur |
Gaussian Blur. This is probably the most common blur filter in
Photoshop. The Blur category has a Blur filter (and also a Blur
More filter), but they just apply a set amount of Blur without
giving you any say in the matter. On the other hand, Gaussian
Blur (named for mathematician Carl Friedrich Gauss) allows
you to control how much blur is applied.

Tip

If you want to apply a blur to a certain part of your image, select it before applying the effect. Then the effect will only affect the selected areas.

FIGURE **13-4** The options for the Gaussian Blur filter

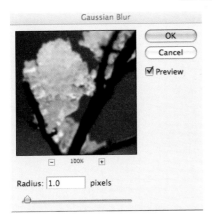

After selecting Gaussian Blur, you will be presented with a simple dialog box (see Figure 13-4) that contains the options for the Gaussian Blur filter.

As you can see, this is a very simple effect. The Radius value is the amount of blur to be applied to the image. A few other features here are common to many other effects. Selecting the Preview check box will allow you to see the results of the blur on the entire image in the main document window in Photoshop without applying it. If this option is unchecked, you can compare and contrast the affected preview in the options dialog with the unaffected image in the main document window. Click OK to apply the effect (see Figure 13-5).

FIGURE **13-5** The result of applying the Gaussian Blur effect, with a Radius value of 4

You can also click and hold in the filter preview window to see the unaffected image. This is perhaps the best way to see a quick before-and-after.

The Gaussian Blur effect is useful in so many instances. As you can see in Figure 13-5, the blur softened the entire image. This creates the illusion that the image is entirely in the background. This illusion makes it easier to add text or other graphic elements on top without the background image being too distracting. You can also blur a layer of flat color (like a layer used as a picture frame), and since there is no definition in the object, you will just be blurring the edges. Or, you can even select a layer mask and apply Gaussian Blur to the mask to soften its edges.

Other types of blurs are worth noting. You can use Motion Blur to blur a layer in a particular direction (controlled with the Angle property in the Motion Blur settings dialog box). This is useful for creating the effect that something is moving quickly through the image (see Figure 13-6).

FIGURE 13-6 The image with Motion Blur applied

The other standout blur effect is Radial Blur. The two main settings for the Blur Method value in this effect's settings radically affect the result. The default setting is Spin, which creates the illusion that the object is being tossed around in a high-powered dryer, as shown in Figure 13-7.

Figure 13-7 The image with Radial Blur applied and Blur Method set to Spin

Tip   With some blur effects, the edges of the layer become blurred, and you will begin to see the transparency grid beneath the layer. That's not good. You can fix it by simply duplicating the layer—CTRL-J (Windows)/CMD-J (Mac). The semi-transparent edges will become more opaque as they are stacked on top of other semi-transparent pixels. You can continue to stack duplicates until the layer is completely opaque.

The other Blur Method setting for the Radial Blur effect is Zoom. As you can see in Figure 13-8, this effect simulates an object zooming toward you, almost like what outer-space travelers see at warp speed.

FIGURE 13-8 The image with Radial Blur applied, Amount set to 50, and Blur Method set to Zoom

Distort Filters

The filters found in the Distort subcategory warp, pull, stretch, and otherwise deform a layer. Filters like Ocean Ripple (Filters | Distort | Ocean Ripple) are good for creating the illusion that we're actually looking at this image through a window on a rainy day, or through privacy doors on a shower, or at a reflection of the image in water (see Figure 13-9).

Of course, if you're looking for a pond-ripple distortion, you'll actually want to use the ZigZag filter. You can find ZigZag by going to Filter | Distort | ZigZag. The Amount value controls the intensity of the ripple, and Ridges determines how many ripples are in the virtual water. Figure 13-10 shows my image with ZigZag applied, the Amount value set to 48, and the Ridges value set to 7.

Note The ultimate distort filter is a plug-in effect called Liquify. We'll look at this effect a little later when we cover warping.

Figure 13-9 Distort filters like Ocean Ripple warp pixels in an image.

Render Filters

Finally in our whirlwind tour of Photoshop's extensive library of filters, we must look at the Render filters. The Render filters all make stuff from scratch, which creates some really interesting possibilities. Many times, these filters don't look impressive on their own, but can be used as the starting point to make some beautiful textures and artwork. I like to think of these filters as flour. On its own, flour isn't special or tasty. But you've probably had some delicious bread or cookies in which flour played a significant role. The Clouds filter is a great example of this. It really doesn't look anything like clouds, but can be used to make a lot of great textures.

Fibers is another filter (like Clouds) that we'll look at more a little later. It creates fibrous textures from scratch, completely replacing the layer that the Fibers filter is applied to. Fibers is used for creepy textures as well as for the basis for wood patterns and other textures (see Figure 13-11). The Fibers filter creates textures

FIGURE 13-10 My image with the ZigZag filter applied

FIGURE 13-11 The Fibers filter, colorized by a Hue/Saturation adjustment layer

using the foreground and background colors, so you'll need to plan for that before applying the effect, or use an adjustment such as Hue/Saturation if you want to adjust the colors.

The Lens Flare effect is a common one that simulates the glare often seen in pictures taken with the sun at certain angles. But Lens Flares can also be used for other purposes as well. In Figure 13-12, I put the Lens Flare over a spot in the ice that was already bright to give the impression that something semi-nuclear is going on inside the ice crystals.

Tip I usually prefer to make a new blank layer, fill it with black, apply the Lens Flare filter to that, and then put that layer into the Screen blend mode. Having the flare on a separate layer gives you more control for blending, selection, and repositioning.

FIGURE **13-12** My image with a Lens Flare filter applied

The last effect in this section I want to cover is the Lighting Effects filter. Apply the Lighting Effects filter by going to Filter | Render | Lighting Effects. This is a big filter, almost like a mini-program. Just look at all of these options shown in Figure 13-13!

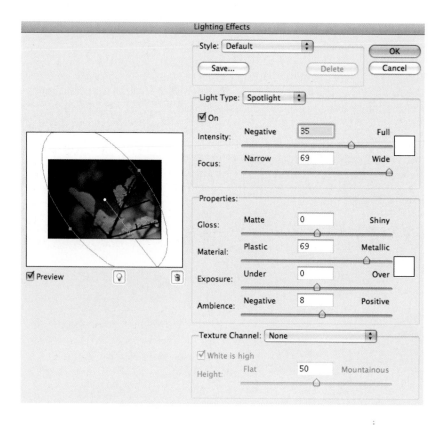

FIGURE 13-13　The Lighting Effects dialog box

This filter adds the effect of a light (or lights) shining on a layer. It has controls for the type of light (for example, spotlight, omni, or directional), the light color, intensity, and much more. If this is all too overwhelming, you can select one of the many presets already created for you in the Style drop-down at the top of this dialog box. Lighting Effects are also great for adding realism to computer-generated images and textures such as the ones we make in Photoshop. Figure 13-14 shows what this effect looks like when applied to my image.

FIGURE **13-14** The results of applying the Lighting Effects filter

Smart Filters

One of the biggest problems with filters was that they were destructive. Once the filter was applied, it was there for good. You could undo the filter immediately after you applied it, but once you closed the document, the filter was permanent. Elsewhere in Photoshop, most other features are (or are becoming) nonpermanent, or nondestructive. We can always change or remove applied layer styles. If we use adjustment layers, we can change or remove color adjustments. Layer masks are nondestructive. Vector shape layers are nondestructive, and the list goes on.

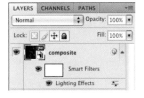

FIGURE **13-15** When filters are applied to a Smart Object, the filters appear underneath the layer, so you can edit them later.

The good news is that filters can be applied nondestructively to Smart Objects. Simply convert a layer to a Smart Object before applying filters, and any filters applied to the Smart Object show up as layer elements in the Layers panel (see Figure 13-15).

Tip   You can also convert a layer to a Smart Object by going to the Filter menu and selecting Convert For Smart Filters (Smart Filters are filters applied to Smart Objects).

To edit applied filters, just double-click the name of the filter in the Layers panel. The same options dialog box that you saw when you applied the effect will show up again with all of your settings intact. To delete a filter, just drag it from the layer to the trash can icon at the bottom of the Layers panel.

You can even adjust how the filter blends into the layer. Just double-click the icon to the right of the name of an applied filter in the Layers panel. A small Blending Options dialog box will pop up that will allow you to fade the effect by reducing its opacity, or to blend the effect into the original layer by using blend modes. Figure 13-16 shows this dialog box, as well as the result of blending the Lighting Effects filter with my original layer using the Overlay blend mode.

FIGURE 13-16 The Blending Options dialog box and the result of the blend

Finally, you might have also noticed a little white square next to the words "Smart Filters" in the Layers panel. That white square is akin to a layer mask for the filters that you apply. Just as with layer masks, you can paint with black to remove areas of the effect. Let's say you were using a Distort filter to simulate pond ripples in a photo of water along the shore. You probably wouldn't want the shore to ripple, so you could mask out the shore area on the Smart Filters mask.

Warping

Now, we'll switch gears a bit, and talk about how to warp images. One of these methods we discussed in Chapter 11, when we looked at warping text. Here, we'll talk about two other methods: the Free Transform warp and the Liquify filter. For these examples, we'll use the art shown in Figure 13-17, which was created by Will Kindrick—a good friend of mine, a terrific illustrator, a fantastic drummer, and an artist on the zany Nick Jr. show, *Yo Gabba Gabba!*

FIGURE 13-17 Art from Will Kindrick that I'll be warping

The Free Transform Warp

Enter Free Transform mode by selecting a layer and using the keyboard shortcut CTRL-T (Windows)/CMD-T (Mac). Then right-click in the main document window on the object. From the right-click menu that pops up, choose Warp. This will create a simple mesh around your object that you can move around to warp the layer (see Figure 13-18).

Once you're in Free Transform mode, a warp icon will show up on the right side of the Options bar. You can also enter Free Transform warp by clicking this button.

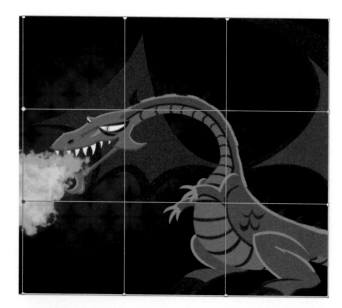

FIGURE 13-18 After you choose to warp your object, a simple grid will appear.

You can pull on the corner points in this grid, or on edges, or on corner handles to distort and pull the pixels on the image beneath it. Using warp, we can distort people's faces, bend dragon wings (see Figure 13-19), take away a couple of pounds (or add them), and much more.

FIGURE 13-19 After we play with the warp mesh a little, our image takes on a different shape.

The Liquify Filter

Most filters reside in subcategories in the Filter menu. But a select few are so powerful that they cannot be confined to categories. They can be found toward the top of the Filter menu, and Liquify is one of those. Liquify is called such because it allows you to warp an image in very organic ways, almost as if your image were turned into water and you were just smearing the water around. For this example, we'll play a round of "Devastatingly Humiliate the Author" with a remarkably unflattering picture of me (see Figure 13-20). I'll select this layer and choose Filter | Liquify.

FIGURE **13-20** The embarrassing image of me, as seen in the Liquify filter

The Liquify filter even has its own set of tools, found in the upper-left area of the interface. The tool selected by default is the Forward Warp tool. This tool is like a smearing tool—just drag with it to smear pixels. You can use this tool to push in a few extra pounds, or reshape features, or anything else you can do by moving pixels around. I'll use this tool to pull up the edges of my mouth, pull up the rest of my mouth a little, and pull down my chin a little bit to channel my inner Jay Leno (see Figure 13-21).

FIGURE 13-21 Me, after using the Forward Warp tool

The next tool is the Reconstruct tool. You can select and paint with this tool to restore liquified pixels to their original state. But I'm just getting warmed up, so I don't want to use it now.

The two other tools I use all the time with this effect are the Pucker tool and the Bloat tool. Holding down the mouse button over pixels when you have the Pucker tool will shrink the areas around your mouse. A more descriptive name for this tool might be the "vacuum" tool, as it appears to suck neighboring pixels toward itself. The Bloat tool does the opposite—it creates the illusion that there is a bubble underneath the pixels that you bloat with this tool. In Figure 13-22, you can see my final results after I used the Bloat tool on my eyes, and the Pucker tool on my nose.

 Liquify can't be applied to Smart Objects. I recommend duplicating your layer and then applying Liquify to the duplicate so that your original layer remains untarnished.

FIGURE 13-22 My final Liquify results. This actually might be an improvement.

Making Textures from Scratch

Now that we've seen what some filters do, let's combine them to create some simple textures from scratch. These will be quick "laundry list" tutorials that will help give you a sense of what filters can do when combined.

Making Metal

First, let's create a 3D metal texture. Create a new Photoshop document at the default Photoshop size (using the preset). Make sure that the background layer is filled with white, and then convert the background layer to a Smart Object. Next, apply Filter | Noise | Add Noise. This filter adds a bunch of junky looking noise. It's great for making a TV screen with bad reception, but not for much else without some adjustment. I'm using this filter in this tutorial so that you can see how even the ugliest of filters can be important when used in a good recipe. Use the noise settings found in Figure 13-23.

Next, choose Filter | Blur | Motion Blur. Use the settings found in Figure 13-24. The metal is starting to look good. But lighting is almost always the key to a good fake, so we'll fix that in the final step.

Finally, we'll add the Lighting Effects filter, found in Filter | Render | Lighting Effects. Use the settings displayed in Figure 13-25. At the bottom of the Lighting Effects filter is a Texture Channel section. You can use that drop-down to select a channel to create a 3D texture. That will create the appearance of 3D ridges in our case.

The final results for this project are shown in Figure 13-26. Because we applied these filters to a Smart Object layer, you have the freedom to go back to any of these filters and adjust their settings. You can remove them or add more. Now that you've created this metal, you can use it as a textured background for text or anything else you can think of.

Making Wood

We'll now create a wood texture from scratch in the same shotgun style in which we made the 3D metal texture.

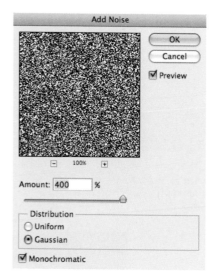

FIGURE 13-23 Use these settings for the Add Noise filter.

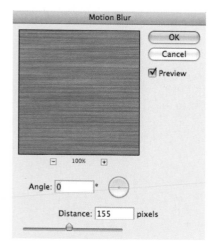

FIGURE 13-24 The settings for the Motion Blur filter

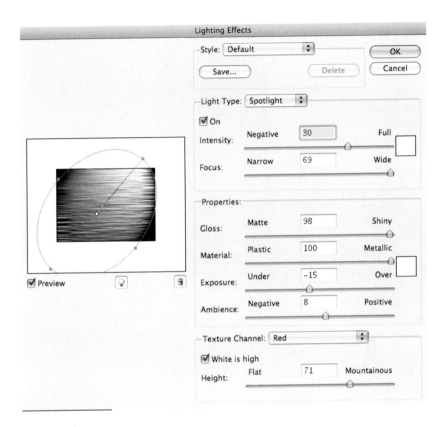

FIGURE **13-25** The settings for the Lighting Effects filter

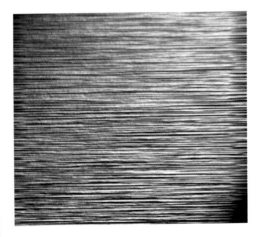

FIGURE **13-26** The final 3D metal result

Make a new Photoshop document at the default size, and make sure the background layer is filled with white and converted to a Smart Object layer. Then apply the Fibers effect found in Filter | Render | Fibers, and use the settings shown in Figure 13-27.

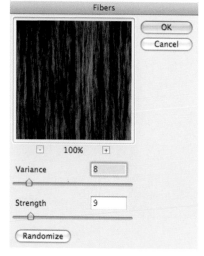

FIGURE 13-27 Use these settings when applying the Fibers filter.

Next, we need to use the Liquify filter, but we can't use it on Smart Objects. Select the layer and duplicate it. Then right-click the duplicate and choose Rasterize Layer. Now apply Filter | Liquify. One of the Liquify tools we haven't covered yet is the Twirl Clockwise tool (third from the top in the Liquify tools area). Clicking and holding this tool will cause neighboring pixels to swirl around your cursor. Use this to create a knot in the wood, as seen in Figure 13-28.

 You can also use the Brush tool shortcuts (the [and] keys on your keyboard) to shrink and increase the size of the tools in the Liquify window.

FIGURE 13-28 Use the Twirl Clockwise tool in the Liquify tools to create a knot in the wood.

The knot looks all right, but the center of it looks too digital and too bright. So, let's select the Burn tool in the Tools panel to darken it. The Burn tool looks like a hand doing a shadow figure, and it's in the same tool slot as the Dodge tool. The Dodge tool—found about halfway down the Tools panel—is displayed by default and looks like a lollipop. Using the Burn tool, drag on the knot to darken it. I also darkened the area around it a little bit to help it blend in better (see Figure 13-29).

Our texture is starting to shape up, but it's missing perhaps the greatest element of all—color. Go to the Adjustments panel, and apply a Hue/Saturation adjustment by clicking the icon with three tiny horizontal bars. The most important option here is Colorize at the bottom

Figure 13-29 The texture after darkening with the Burn tool

of the Adjustments panel. This tells Hue/Saturation to add color where none exists, which is the case here. I took the Hue value to an orange color and increased the saturation. I also added another instance of the Lighting Effects filter to create the final wood texture (see Figure 13-30). Not too shabby, considering that we created this from scratch in a few short steps!

Figure 13-30 The final wood texture

Creating Fine Art

Finally in this chapter, I want to show you that you can use filters in interesting ways to create beautiful art. By now, you're very familiar with the process of applying filters and color adjustments, so I'll go through this rather quickly. Don't get concerned with what buttons I'm pushing here. This is more of a creative ideas workshop. I'm starting where I've started with the other projects in this chapter—with a new Photoshop document at the default size with a white background layer converted to a Smart Object. Next, I'll apply Filter | Render | Clouds (see Figure 13-31).

Then I'll apply Filter | Texture | Patchwork. This turns our image into a series of squares, as if it were a quilt, as shown in Figure 13-32.

FIGURE 13-31   The Clouds filter

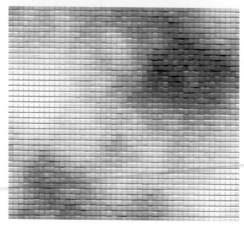

FIGURE 13-32   The Patchwork filter applied to Clouds

Next, I'll apply Filter | Distort | Polar Coordinates, which will wrap this layer around itself in a circle. As you can see in Figure 13-33, a noticeable seam is at the top where the two edges meet. We could easily fix that with the Clone Stamp tool, but we won't take the time to do that here.

This is finally starting to look a little artistic. I'll add a Levels adjustment and a Color Balance adjustment. I fiddled with the settings until I found the colors that I liked (see Figure 13-34).

We could end it here, but the magic is in adding more filters. So, what if we added Filter | Blur | Radial Blur with the Blur Method set to Zoom? Let's do it (see Figure 13-35).

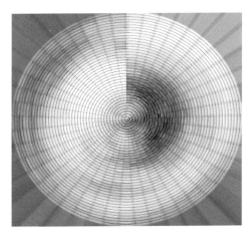

FIGURE 13-33 The art after applying Polar Coordinates

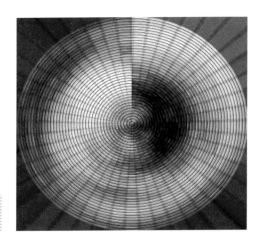

FIGURE 13-34 The art after adding color

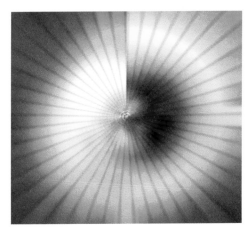

FIGURE 13-35 The art after adding even more effects

The point here is to just have fun and to experiment. Think something looks interesting? Try dumping a Radial Blur filter on it. Try changing its color. Try creating interesting paint strokes and then applying filters to the strokes. The possibilities are endless, bounded only by your creativity.

14

Advanced Creative Concepts

How to...

- Use layer comps
- Create a 3D eyeball from scratch
- Work with guides
- Create custom brushes
- Find additional Photoshop presets online

As you've probably seen by now, being good at Photoshop really means being creative. In this chapter, we'll revisit the idea of creativity. We'll look at even more ways to be creative, including using layer comps, which allow you to quickly see different versions of your designs.

Throughout this book, we've been learning loads of useful features. But the individual features of Photoshop really reach their peak when used together. So, in this chapter, we'll also look at how to combine many of the Photoshop features we've learned about separately (brushes, filters, and so on) to make a very eye-popping project. (We'll be making an eyeball, so that was a foreshadowing joke.)

We'll also look a little at customizing Photoshop. Though we'll save the bulk of this discussion for Chapter 16, we'll look here at how to create your own brushes. This is much more useful than it sounds. It's such a great feature, in fact, that people make and distribute (or sometimes sell) all over the Internet the brushes and other Photoshop presets that they create. I'll also show you some of my favorite places to go for extras.

Using Layer Comps

One of the things that used to be very frustrating to designers (and is still frustrating to them when not using Photoshop) is that they often need to be able to see multiple versions of their designs at once. They might be unsure about what design they want to go with, or they may want to give their clients some options. The Layer Comps panel is the solution to this problem. When you create a layer comp, you save certain states of your document that you can instantly return to at any time. You can have certain layers visible in one of the comps, or in certain positions, or with certain layer styles, and save that state as a layer comp. You can then adjust things like layer visibility, position, and layer styles, and create another layer comp. Let's see how this works.

I'm working with the design seen in Figure 14-1. This is a mock poster of an ad for a kid playing Guitar Hero live in Seattle that we've been working on throughout this book. I'm unsure if I like the layer styles applied to the photo of the boy. A Color Overlay effect is applied to colorize the photo so that it matches the sign color below it. Also, a Stroke effect creates the black outline around the photo. I'm also unsure if I like the placement of the elements.

FIGURE 14-1 The original layout

FIGURE **14-2** The Layer Comps panel

Now, let's see what this layout looks like with some adjustments. But before doing that, save this current layout by using a layer comp. To do that, go to the Window menu and open the Layer Comps panel. Click the Create New Layer Comp button (next to the trash can icon) at the bottom of the panel to save this layout in its current state as a layer comp (see Figure 14-2).

After clicking the Create New Layer Comp button, you'll be presented with a dialog box (see Figure 14-3) that allows you to save a lot of descriptive information about the layer comp, to name it, and to tell Photoshop what aspects of the current layout you'd like it to remember. It's a good idea to name it something descriptive as well, especially if you plan on having several layer comps. That way you can instantly tell at a glance which layer comp is which in the Layer Comps panel.

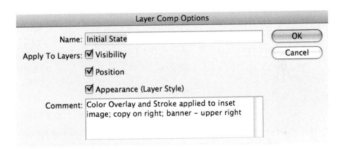

FIGURE **14-3** The options for a layer comp

Now that this current layout is saved as a layer comp, I can experiment knowing that my initial layout is still instantly accessible at any time. I'll change around the position of my layers, and adjust the layer styles applied to the image of the kid. Figure 14-4 shows my changes.

Now, if I want to go back to the first layout, I can simply click the little square next to the name of the layer comp in the Layer Comps panel. Or I can click the left and right arrows at the bottom of the Layers Comps panel to go back and forth. In this way, you can see wildly different designs instantly, which makes it much easier to choose between them.

To go back to the current working layout, click the square next to Last Document State.

This Friday, come watch the legendary child aLorem ipsum dolor sit amet, consectetuer adipiscing elit, sed diam nonummy nibh euismod tincidunt ut laoreet dolore magna aliquam erat volutpat. Ut wisi enim ad minim veniam, quis nostrud exerci tation ullamcorper suscipit lobortis nisl ut aliquip ex ea commodo consequat. Duis autem vel eum iriure dolor in hendrerit in vulputate velit esse molestie consequat, vel illum dolore eu feugiat nulla facilisis at vero eros et accumsan et iusto odio dignissim qui blandit praesent luptatum zzril delenit augue duis dolore te feugait nulla facilisi.

FIGURE 14-4 My document, after making various changes to the design

Project: Bringing It All Together

We'll now create a sample project that uses multiple features. My purpose here is to stimulate your creative muscles. We'll be creating a realistic eye texture from scratch, and then we'll wrap it around a 3D sphere, which will create a real 3D eyeball that you can move and rotate in 3D. In the course of this big project, we'll be reviewing and practicing many of the features we've already learned about, but we'll also be learning a few new ones.

Create the Document

The first step is to create a new Photoshop document using the default size preset; make sure that the background layer is white. We need to make the pupil of the eye in the center of the document, but exactly where is that? We need some guides to help us set that up, so we'll do that in the next step.

Creating Guides

When you drive a car on most major highways, lines on the ground let you know where your lane is. The lines don't really do anything to prevent you from crossing them—they're just there to indicate boundaries. Guides in Photoshop do the same thing. Guides are light blue lines that we can use to help keep our work lined up.

Here, we want to place the eye in the center of the document. We could figure it out with rulers, but we'll use many layers to create this eye. We definitely don't want to make those same measurements over and over again for every layer that needs to be centered. Guides are the answer here.

Don't worry—guides don't show up in the final image when you export it.

To create guides, we first need to look at our rulers. As with guides, rulers and other such helpers can be displayed and controlled via the View menu. Go to View | Rulers to display the rulers on the top and left side of your document. Notice the tiny, faint line that displays on the rulers as you move your mouse. This lets you know exactly where your mouse is.

Right-click the rulers to select a new system of measurement (pixels, inches, and so on).

Make sure that your system of measurement is inches. Next, select the Move tool in the Tools panel. Drag down from the ruler at the top of the document to create a horizontal guide. Looking at the line created by your cursor on the left ruler as a reference, drag this guide down 2.5" (half the height of our document). From the ruler along the left edge, drag out a guide. Use the top ruler as a reference to create a vertical guide at 3.5" (half the width of our document). See Figure 14-5.

If you find that you're accidentally moving the guides around, you can go to View | Lock Guides to prevent them from being moved.

FIGURE 14-5 The document with guides

Making the Eye

The first step in making the eye itself is to create a blank new layer. Then select the Elliptical marquee tool in the Tools panel. Make a circular selection that roughly matches the size and location of the circle seen in Figure 14-6 (about 1" in diameter). Press D to reset the default colors. Then use the keyboard shortcut ALT-BACKSPACE (Windows)/OPTION-DELETE (Mac) to fill the blank layer with black.

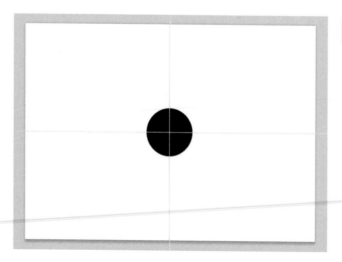

FIGURE 14-6 The black circle

Next, create another new blank layer. We want to create a similar circle on this layer, but we want it to be filled with green. Click the foreground color swatch at the bottom of the Tools panel, and select a green color (or whatever color you want your eye to be) from the Color Picker. We want another elliptical selection, but we want it to be the same size as the black circle we just created. So, with the new blank layer selected, CTRL-click (Windows)/CMD-click (Mac) the layer thumbnail of the black layer. If you do this correctly, the new blank layer will stay selected, and the selection area will exactly match the black circle you just created. Use the same keyboard shortcut to fill this layer with green. You should now have three layers: a white background layer, the black circle layer, and the green circle layer.

Right-click the green circle layer, and select Convert To Smart Object. We'll be adding some filters to this layer, and by converting it to a Smart Object, you can change the settings later. With the green circle layer selected, choose Filter | Noise | Add Noise. Use **60** for the Amount setting with both Gaussian and Monochromatic selected. As seen in Figure 14-7, this should now look like a really ugly Petri dish.

Next, apply Filter | Blur | Radial Blur to the green circle layer. Change the Blur Method to Zoom, the Amount to about **70**, and the quality to Best (see Figure 14-8).

Next, we'll scale down the green circle layer a little. Enter Free Transform mode by selecting the green circle layer and pressing CTRL-T (Windows)/CMD-T (Mac). Drag a corner point of the bounding box while holding the keyboard shortcut SHIFT-ALT (Windows)/SHIFT-OPTION (Mac). Now our project is starting to look a little like an eye (see Figure 14-9).

The eye is looking better, but the colors are too uniform. Adding chaos and randomness is usually the secret to making computer-generated images look more realistic. This next step will add a lot more realism. Duplicate the green circle layer by selecting the layer and pressing CTRL-J (Windows)/CMD-J (Mac). We want to turn the copy that is on top in the Layers panel to a different color. For this, go to Image | Adjustments | Variations (see Figure 14-10). This allows you to see your layer with variations of color. The top area shows you the original layer and the new, changed version. As you click any of the color spots around the original, you'll change the color. I'll click More Blue, and then click More Cyan, and click OK to accept my changes. This color adjustment is somewhat special in that

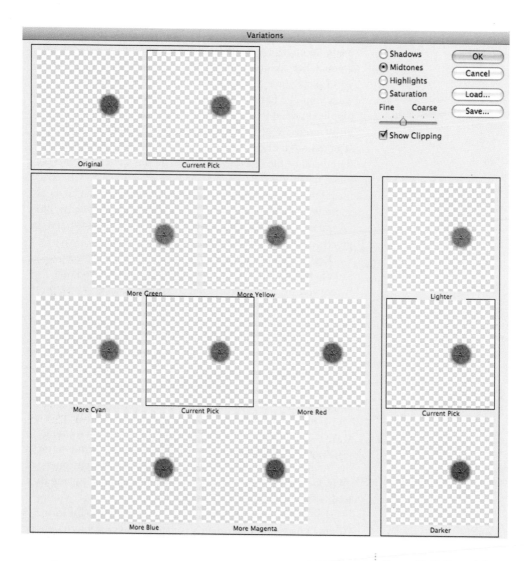

FIGURE 14-10 The copied green circle layer, adjusted in Variations

it is a color adjustment that can be applied nondestructively to a Smart Object layer. As with filters, once you've applied Variations, you can double-click the word "Variations" on your layer to open your settings and make changes.

Now, take down the opacity of the bluish layer we've just adjusted to about **60** so it blends in with the green. It looks much better, but we still need more randomness. So, on the bluish circle layer, double-click the Add Noise effect to adjust the filter we've previously applied. The Add Noise filter options

FIGURE **14-11** After adding colored noise to the bluish layer

FIGURE **14-12** The completed eye texture

FIGURE **14-13** The squashed texture

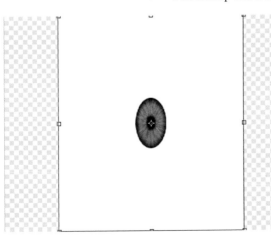

will pop up. Change the Amount of noise to about **30**, and uncheck Monochromatic, so that we get a few random colors in there as well. Now we're starting to create a more natural look (see Figure 14-11).

We're almost done. Let's finish this by creating the pupil. Create another new blank layer. Make a small elliptical marquee selection and fill it with black. You can convert this layer to a Smart Object if you wish. Apply Filter | Blur | Gaussian Blur, and set the Radius value to **6**. The texture is now complete, as shown in Figure 14-12.

Preparing the Eye to Be a 3D Texture

Now, we need to prepare this texture to be applied to a 3D object. Photoshop can apply multiple layers as a 3D texture, but we'll combine, or merge, these layers together into one. *Merging* is a process where we combine several layers so that they can operate as a single layer. We *could* go to the fly-out menu of the Layers panel and choose Flatten Image, which would combine all layers into a single image. But then we couldn't go back and adjust individual layers. We're looking for the best of all worlds here—to use all of these layers as one layer, and to have the ability to edit them later if we choose to. Here's the trick. Use the finger-tangling keyboard shortcut CTRL-ALT-SHIFT-E (Windows)/CMD-OPTION-SHIFT-E (Mac). This will make a new blank layer and paste a copy of all layers merged together onto that layer.

One final step is needed before adding this to a 3D object. Photoshop has a tendency to stretch textures, and the current version doesn't give us the option to manually adjust the way textures are applied to 3D objects. So, we need to compensate for the stretching that will occur. Enter Free Transform mode. While holding the ALT/OPTION key, drag one of the points along the left or right edge of the bounding box, and drag toward the center to squash the composite image layer (see Figure 14-13); click ENTER on the numeric keypad to accept the transformation.

Creating the 3D Object

Now we're ready to finish this project. Select the squashed composite texture layer. Choose 3D | New Shape From Layer | Sphere. You've just created an eyeball! (See Figure 14-14.) Good job!

FIGURE 14-14 The final eyeball project

How to... Add Final Touches

You might have noticed in Figure 14-14 that I added a couple final touches. In real life, eyes are a little slimy and moist, so light bounces off them as it would a marble. To re-create this effect, you can select the 3D layer, and then go to the Materials tab of the 3D panel. Increase the Glossiness value to increase the brightness of the highlights. Increase the Shininess value to decrease the size of the highlights, making the object appear shinier.

Creating Custom Brushes

Textures add so much to our work in Photoshop, especially in light of current design trends. Because of this, it really pays to be able to create your own custom brushes. In the next couple of paragraphs, we'll look at how to do this and why it's so cool.

First, open an image that has some interesting textures in it. I'll use an image of an insect. One of the great things about brushes is that they can contain 256 shades of gray. You can actually create brushes out of black-and-white images. The image I have open is shown in Figure 14-15.

FIGURE **14-15** The insect image

Next, I'll go to Edit | Define Brush Preset. Now, when I use the Brush tool and right-click to see my library of brushes, this insect brush will be available (at the bottom of the list) to use. When I paint with this, it creates a stamp of the original image. Notice that the areas in the insect image that were lighter are more transparent, allowing the green to show through. Darker pixels in the image are more opaque when the image is converted to a brush. Figure 14-16 shows the result of my painting with black, red, and white on a green background. The effect is like creating a stamp with the insect image. Notice their transparency as they overlap.

FIGURE **14-16** After painting with the newly created insect brush on a green background

Before creating custom brushes, I usually apply Levels to make dark areas more dark (opaque) and light areas more light (transparent).

Let's look at one more example. This time, I'll customize my brush further before creating it. For this example, I'll reuse a fireworks photograph from when we looked at cloning. I'm choosing the image in Figure 14-17 because it has some truly fantastic texture.

FIGURE 14-17 The fireworks image we'll be using to make a new brush

When you make a new brush, it's a good idea to adjust it if you're not going for photorealism (like we saw with the insect brush). For this fireworks brush, I want to use these sparks to create some grunge on another photo, but I don't really want the fireworks to be obvious. So, I'll add a Levels adjustment. This will get rid of the smoky haze in the middle of the image and will make the sparks brighter (see Figure 14-18). As a result, the sparks will be more opaque when the image is converted to a brush.

FIGURE 14-18 The fireworks image after a Levels adjustment

Technically, this Levels adjustment will make the sparks more transparent, because "white" means "transparent." So, after clicking OK on the Levels adjustment, I'll add an Invert adjustment, which will flip black and white. Next, I'll add an adjustment called Threshold, which forces every pixel to be either pure black or pure white. This effect is great for creating edgy art. Adjust the Threshold level to control the range of pixels that turn black or white. After adding all three adjustments (Levels, Invert, and Threshold), we should have something that makes for terrible fireworks but a fantastic custom brush (see Figure 14-19).

Before we make this image a brush, we must put this onto one layer. If we select the background layer to create the brush, the brush would look like the original image without the adjustments we've applied. So, we need to flatten this image. As with the eye project, create a new layer, select it, and press CTRL-ALT-SHIFT-E (Windows)/CMD-OPTION-SHIFT-E (Mac) to merge the final result onto one layer. Then select Edit | Define Brush Preset.

FIGURE 14-19 The fireworks
image after all adjustments

 You can also make a selection with any of the selection tools to define a portion of your image as a brush preset.

Next, I'll open another image to paint on with my new brush. After applying paint strokes with my new custom brush on different layers (one with white paint, one with black paint), changing the brush size, and varying the opacity of the paint layers, the results are intense. It's a great way to add some extra emotion to a design or photograph, as you can see in Figure 14-20.

FIGURE **14-20** An image painted with our fireworks brush

Finding More Photoshop Presets

Photoshop presets are such a blast to use—whether to create a certain look or just to experiment. A couple of great resources on the Internet offer loads of content—most of it free.

The first is the Adobe Studio Exchange. As of this writing, the address is www.adobe.com/cfusion/exchange. Unfortunately, Adobe doesn't seem to prize this resource as much as it should. The site address changes quite often. So, if it's no longer here, just do a Google search (or an adobe.com search) for Adobe Studio Exchange.

The Adobe Studio Exchange (see Figure 14-21) is a community of users who share custom presets with each other. It astounds me how generous some of these artists are. From this site, you can download additional layer styles, brushes, shapes, actions, patterns, and much more. Most of it is free, and much of it can be used for commercial purposes.

Another great creative community is deviantart.com. This site also has many presets and images that you can download from other artists. It has a more artistic community than the community on the Adobe site, and it's not just for sharing Photoshop content.

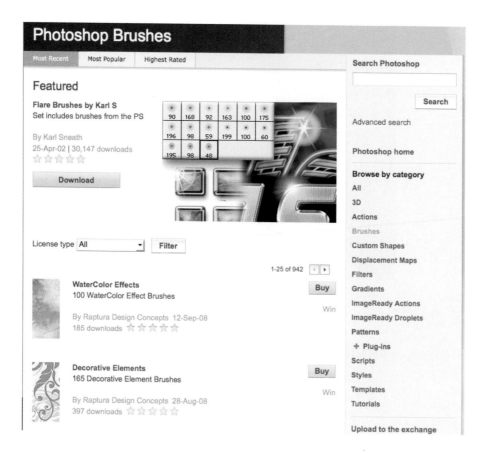

FIGURE 14-21 The Brushes area of the Adobe Studio Exchange

One of my favorite sites is good-tutorials.com, which doesn't supply presets. But it does have loads and loads of fantastic Photoshop tutorials that you can use to create your own presets.

Finally, whenever you're looking for anything related to Photoshop—be it a preset or a troubleshooting question—the best resource of all is Google. You can find anything you're looking for through Google, so never underestimate it!

15
Exporting

How to...

- Print images
- Export files to the Web
- Export files to page layout programs
- Export files to cell phones and mobile devices

Now that you know how to make a masterpiece, what do you do with it? In this chapter, we'll look at how to export your work in Photoshop. Back when I first started learning Photoshop, this discussion was very simple. The road of exporting led to one destination: printing. In today's technology climate, however, we output to print, the Web, cell phones and other mobile devices, 3D, and video. In Chapter 12, we covered how to export to 3D and video. In this chapter, we'll look at how to print documents and how to export them for the Web and mobile devices. While looking at the features of Photoshop that pertain to mobile devices, you'll also be introduced to another application that ships for free with Photoshop (as Bridge does), Device Central.

Printing and Exporting

The most common way of getting Photoshop documents off of your computer is to print them. This might mean printing to a desktop inkjet printer, to a professional printing service that uses million-dollar equipment, or to everything in between.

You can output to print in a few different ways. You can print directly from Photoshop, or you can save your Photoshop document in another format that can be used in a page layout program (such as Adobe InDesign) to be printed from there. Page layout programs usually have more sophisticated printing options than Photoshop has.

The Print Dialog Box

First, let's look at how to print directly from Photoshop. Go to
File | Print to open the newly redesigned Print dialog box, which
you can see in Figure 15-1. These settings are now much more
self-explanatory, but I want to cover a few options that aren't so
obvious at the outset.

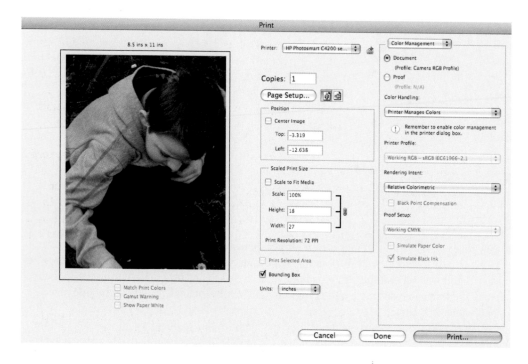

FIGURE 15-1 The Print dialog box

If your printer driver has certain features, you can access
those settings by clicking the little printer-and-crosshairs icon
at the top center of the dialog box, next to the Printer selection
drop-down. You can also click the Page Setup button to change
the size of paper you're outputting to. If you want to print a
portion of your image, deselect the Center Image check box
to have the ability to move your image around. When you've
completed adjusting your settings, click the Print button to print
the document. If you just want to save those settings for later,
click Done.

Choosing a File Format

"What file format should I use?" is a question I hear frequently. People who are new to Photoshop often look at the list of possible output formats and feel intimidated. Yes, the volume of choices available when outputting files is massive. The good news is that you don't have to know what every choice does. Chances are, most of the output file formats will never come in handy for you.

This feeling of being overwhelmed by output options also extends to being overwhelmed at all of the tools in the Tools panel, or all of the other programs that people use to do artistic work. The solution to overcoming this intimidated feeling is to realize that you only need to know what you need to know. The most common output file format for images when going to a page layout program is TIFF. For printing, it doesn't matter what the other formats do. If your printing service needs something different, such as a DCS 2.0 EPS, they will let you know. The same holds true for the Web. The most common image format on the Web—by far—is JPEG. There are a few others, of course. But don't obsess about what you *don't* know. A good rule of thumb is that if 90 percent of the world is using a certain standard, no one will fault you for using it.

Exporting to a Page Layout Program

Depending on the page layout program you're using, several output file formats will work. To output to a different file type, go to File | Save As. In the Save As dialog box, click the Format drop-down to see the available output formats. The drop-down lists many formats, but only a few are applicable to page layout and printing. As mentioned, for printing images, the most common image format is TIFF. TIFF files can be in RGB or CMYK, and can contain layers, transparency, and more. It is a *lossless* format, which means that when you save images, it does not degrade them. Contrast that with JPEG, which is probably the most common image format overall. We'll look more at JPEG files in a moment.

When you choose to save your image as a TIFF file, you're presented with the TIFF Options dialog box, shown in Figure 15-2. With options like "Per Channel (RRGGBB) Pixel

Order," this dialog box can be a little scary at first. But you should need to change only a few options from their defaults. For Image Compression at the top, I usually choose either None, which creates an uncompressed image, or LZW, which compresses the image slightly. The other TIFF option that I often use is Layer Compression. If you don't need layers in your TIFF file (and most of the time you don't, because the layers are saved and more accessible in the original PSD file), choose Discard Layers And Save A Copy. This will greatly reduce the size of your file if you have many layers.

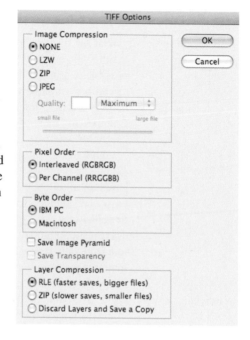

JPEG files are created from many digital cameras, are used often on the Web, and sometimes are used for printing (even though they shouldn't be). JPEG files are considered *lossy*, the opposite of lossless. That means that every time you save a JPEG, you destroy its quality a little. If you must work on a JPEG file, save it first as a PSD file. Then as you continue to work on it, it won't be damaged every time it is saved.

FIGURE 15-2 The TIFF Options dialog box

Another popular format in professional printing is EPS. EPS files can store both raster (pixelated) and vector data. EPS remains popular today because it used to be the standard format for printed files. It is quickly being replaced by Adobe Acrobat's PDF file format. You may have seen PDF files on the Web or at work. Most of the time, the PDF format is just used for online brochures and such. But PDF is actually one of the most powerful and versatile file formats. It also can contain raster and vector data, and is more sophisticated than EPS is.

Note   Some page layout programs, such as InDesign, allow you to import a layered PSD (Photoshop Document) file as is. Because of the flexibility in working with PSD files, I prefer working with them.

Making Print and Onscreen Colors Match

When I teach Photoshop classes, one of the most common questions I get is "how do I make my printed colors match what I see onscreen?" I really feel your pain on this. Sometimes, when you're printing a beautiful landscape image with a deep blue sky, it comes out purple. Or, colors might turn out significantly darker or lighter than they were onscreen. You would think that Photoshop would just have a button that said "Make All Colors Match."

Unfortunately, it's not quite that simple. Photoshop isn't the only player in the color matching game. Other software is involved, such as your operating system and your video card drivers. Hardware such as your monitor and printer are also at work. Any one of these puzzle pieces could be responsible for colors not matching. Entire books have been written on color management, so I won't try to summarize that much information here. But I do want to give you a couple of tips that might help solve some of the biggest problems.

The first tip is that you need to be aware that CMYK (the colors used in printing) is not capable of printing many colors seen in RGB (the colors most commonly used in computer documents). This is especially true of vibrant cool tones such as blue. You can go to View | Proof Setup | Working CMYK to get a general idea of what an image might look like when printed.

The next tip is that you should make sure that your hardware (for example, monitor and printer) is calibrated. If your printer reads things a little dark, then calibration can help it balance things out. Most hardware devices come with their own system of calibration, however pathetic it may be. You can also purchase other calibration utilities if color accuracy is a major issue. A *colorimeter* is a device that can measure the color produced by other devices and adjust them accordingly.

One other thing I recommend is to check Photoshop's Help files on color management. If you've purchased the entire Creative Suite in one package, you can use Adobe Bridge to make sure that all devices in the suite are using consistent color.

Saving for the Web

Saving images for use on the Web has become a world unto itself. So, Adobe has created the Save For Web & Devices dialog box, shown in Figure 15-3. This dialog box is so powerful that it's almost like a mini-application.

Perhaps the most important setting in this dialog box is the easy-to-miss format drop-down below the Preset drop-down in the upper-right area of the dialog box. From this drop-down,

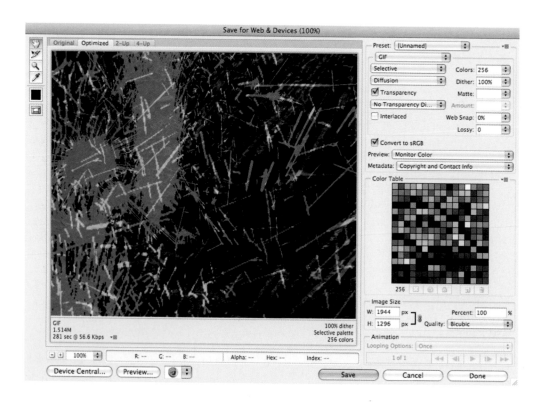

FIGURE 15-3 The Save For Web & Devices dialog box

you can choose which file format to use to save your document. You have five choices: GIF, JPEG, PNG-8, PNG-24, and WBMP (see Figure 15-4). We'll briefly go over all of these so you'll know when to use them.

The GIF File Format

The GIF file format ("giff," with either a hard *G* or a soft *G*), is one of the original web image formats. Outputting to a GIF file is best with areas of flat color such as you might find in a cartoon or in vector art. Images with areas of smooth color transitions such as you see in photographs are better left to the JPEG file format in most instances.

The GIF file format also has a couple of tricks up its sleeves. It can store transparency, and it also can contain animation. In the early days of the Web, before the Flash (SWF) file format came into existence to add more sophistication to web animation, the GIF file format was the only way to bring

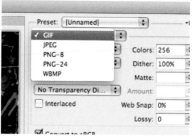

FIGURE 15-4 The format drop-down in the Save For Web & Devices dialog box

life to the Internet. Hence, web sites had far too many tacky animations going on. It was a dark time for us all.

GIF files can contain a maximum of 256 colors. You can reduce or add colors (up to 256) by using the Colors value in the upper-right corner of the Save For Web & Devices dialog box. Fewer colors will result in smaller file sizes (and therefore, quicker download times), but won't usually look as good as GIF files with more colors. For all file formats, you can choose from a series of presets from the Preset drop-down at the top right of the dialog box.

You can compare different presets, and even different file formats, by using the 2-Up and 4-Up tabs on the top left area of the dialog box. The 2-Up tab shows you the original image and a compressed image. The 4-Up tab (see Figure 15-5) shows you the original and three different compressed versions in four squares. You can click to select one of the squares, and then change the format or other settings. Only the settings of the selected square will change. This allows you to see which settings look best when compared with the original.

Figure 15-5 The 4-Up display in the Save For Web & Devices dialog box allows you to compare different types of image compression.

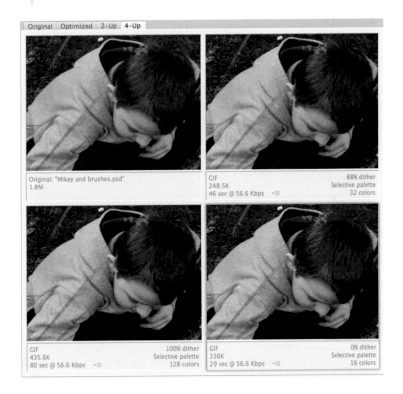

The JPEG File Format

The JPEG file format is really spectacular. I get cranky when I see JPEGs used in printing situations. But the fact of the matter, for the Web at least, is JPEG is still the standard and has been for years. The JPEG file format is meant to compress photos, or graphics with smooth tones like gradients.

With JPEG selected as the format in this dialog box, a quality setting is right below it. You can choose from options like Low, Medium, and High. If you want to get more specific, you can use the Quality slider to the right of the drop-down.

 With JPEG selected as the format, the color table in the bottom right of the dialog box is grayed out. You cannot remove the colors of JPEG files as you can with GIF files.

The PNG File Format

The PNG file format ("ping") comes in two varieties: PNG-8 and PNG-24. The numbers refer to how many colors the formats can contain, in powers of two. So, PNG-8 files can have 256 colors, and PNG-24 files can have 16.7 million colors. Think of PNG-8 files as GIF files and PNG-24 files as JPEG files.

PNG is the native file format for Adobe Fireworks, a program for creating graphics for the Web. PNG files are not as common as GIF and JPEG, and may not be supported in all browsers.

When putting graphics on the Web, I typically prefer GIF and JPEG because the file sizes tend to be smaller, and they have greater compatibility with web browsers. However, PNG-24 files can contain soft-edged transparency. With transparency in GIF files, each pixel is either completely opaque or completely transparent, which creates an ugly, hard edge in most cases. PNG-24 files can create a gradual fade from opaque to transparent. This is one of the few file types that can pull off this feat, and still compress to such a small file size.

The WBMP File Format

The WBMP file format is an old standard for cell phone graphics. "WBMP" is short for "Wireless Bitmap." These files are always black and white, with no shades of gray. Most cell phones and mobile devices support many other formats that are better suited for graphics.

Exporting to Mobile Devices

The dialog box we've been looking at is called Save For Web & Devices because from here, you not only can save your document in web formats, but you can send it to cell phones as well. And I'm not just talking about the superweak WBMP format, either. Photoshop CS4 ships with Device Central, a somewhat new application designed specifically for mobile device content. You can even launch it from this dialog box by clicking the Device Central button in the lower-left corner. This will open Device Central (see Figure 15-6), and you will see the square you had selected in 4-Up view displayed in a cell phone.

FIGURE 15-6 Device Central as launched from the Save For Web & Devices dialog box

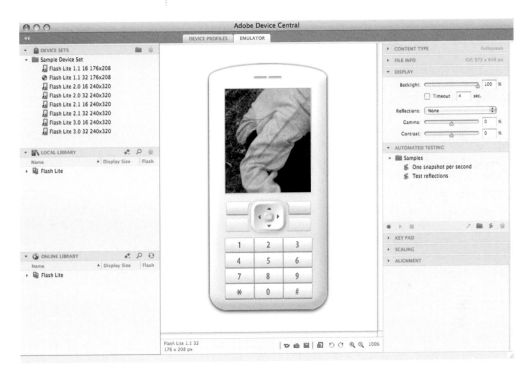

Device Central allows you to download profiles of specific phones and to preview content as it will appear on those phones. You can also browse through various makes and models of phones and view their information at a glance. This includes their pixel dimensions, which version of HTML they support, which image file formats they support, what versions of Flash they support, and more.

By using the Online Library panel in the lower-left corner, you can view all the available cell phone manufacturers and the phones they make. This library is online, so you'll need an Internet connection to access it. To download cell phone images, drag them from the Online Library panel to the Local Library panel right above it. Then you can click an image in the Local Library panel to view your documents in that exact model of cell phone. Probably only about five of you out there will ever try this, but it will make it much easier for you. Device Central also makes it very easy to make content for mobile devices, even for people who have never tried it before.

If you want to create artwork specifically for mobile phones and nothing else, you can launch Device Central, and then from the Welcome screen, choose Create New Mobile | Photoshop File. Then you can select a phone profile, and a Photoshop document that matches the specs of that device will automatically be created for you.

16

Time Savers and Automation

How to...

- Use actions to automate your workflow
- Use actions as tutorials
- Automatically crop and straighten photo scans
- Create a panorama from multiple images
- Save settings in dialog boxes

Usually, chapters on saving time aren't super popular. They just aren't flashy enough, I suppose. But trust me when I say that Photoshop's features to speed up your work are nothing short of spectacular. For example, this chapter will show you how to have Photoshop create an entire web site that shows off your photography—complete with thumbnails, animation, scroll bars, buttons, and more—and how to create all that with a single mouse-click.

We'll first look at the real powerhouse of Photoshop automation: actions. *Actions* are almost like little robots. You "teach" them a series of commands, and then you can click a button at any time and have them automatically execute those commands. Do you find yourself doing the same mundane tasks in Photoshop over and over again? Are all of the photos from your camera a little too red or a little too big? Actions can take care of those headaches for you.

We'll also look at another hidden group of automated Photoshop commands. Finally, we'll look at how to speed up the process of working in most dialog boxes by saving and reusing settings. This chapter will revolutionize the way you work in Photoshop and make you much more efficient (profitable), so let's jump in!

Note An Automation workspace is already created for you in Photoshop. This workspace leaves open the Layers, Channels, and Paths panels, opens the Actions panel, and closes all others. You can access this by going to the workspace drop-down in the upper-right corner of the interface.

Automating with Actions

If you've ever used *macros* in another program (like Microsoft Word), *actions* in Photoshop work in a similar way. They record your actions in Photoshop and can be played back at any time. Let's say that you have a certain size that you scale images down to before posting them to the Web. Maybe there's also a signature color adjustment that you like to add as well. Maybe you use a series of filters to create a certain texture. Maybe you want to create a frame around the edges of your photos. And just maybe you want to do all of these things on multiple images. If you use actions, you only have to perform these steps once; then you can have the action do them for you from that point on.

Photoshop ships with many libraries of actions. You can access actions from the Actions panel. Let's see what one of these default actions does. Open an image to use to test a few of these actions; mine is shown in Figure 16-1.

Tip   If the Actions panel is not visible, you can open it from the Window menu.

Figure 16-1 The image I will be performing actions on

FIGURE **16-2** The Actions panel, with the Default Actions set open

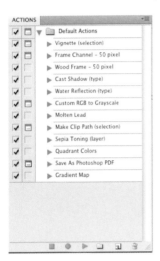

It's important to note that the Actions panel displays groups (or "sets") of actions. The default set of actions is—surprise—Default Actions (see Figure 16-2). The Default Actions set is kind of an actions sampler to give you an idea of the type of things you can do with actions. Click the down arrow next to the name of a set to open it and see all the individual actions within it.

I'll apply the Quadrant Colors action. The Actions panel uses VCR terminology and iconology, so this should seem somewhat familiar. At the bottom of the Actions panel, clicking the circle button allows you to record your actions. Clicking the square stops recording. And clicking the right arrow will play actions. So, click the Quadrant Colors action in the Actions panel, and then click the Play button. It will go through more than a dozen steps to create the result, but it will do so at lightning speed. When it's finished, you will have a monotone image with four separate colors in four separate quadrants, as shown in Figure 16-3.

 Many of the actions that come with Photoshop do you the favor of creating the results on a brand-new layer. That way, if you don't like the result, you can just throw the layer away and there's no harm done for experimenting.

FIGURE **16-3** The result of applying the Quadrant Colors action to my image

As with brushes, we can load new actions libraries from the Actions panel by going to the Actions panel's fly-out menu, shown in Figure 16-4. You can choose from such categories as Image Effects (actions to apply to images for a stylized look), Textures (combinations of filters and effects to create textures from scratch), and more. You can also load actions from somewhere else on your hard drive (or actions that you've purchased, or actions that you've downloaded from the Adobe Studio Exchange mentioned in Chapter 14, or from anywhere else). You can load them by choosing Load Actions from this fly-out menu.

FIGURE 16-4 The Actions panel menu

Did You Know?

Some Selections Are Different

Some selections have interesting little quirks. In the presets that ship with Photoshop, these quirks are indicated in the name of the action. Some have "(selection)" at the end of their names. This indicates that the action will apply to a selected area, and thus, you must have an active selection when using the action in order for it to work properly.

Some actions have "(type)" after their names. This indicates that the action is designed to be applied to text. For these actions to work properly, text must be created and the text layer selected before applying the action.

If you forget or are unsure of what extra steps are required by an action, but apply it anyway, you will usually get an error message saying that such and such command is not available. At that point, you can continue the action without that step, or you can stop the action.

Finally, remember to take a page out of the Adobe notebook. When you create your own selections, it's a really good idea to give them names to remind you of any special instructions. This can be especially helpful if you want to share your actions with other users.

Use Actions as Tutorials

Each individual action in every set of actions has its own down arrow. If you click that down arrow, you will see all the commands that make up that particular action.

Because of this neat little detail, you can use actions to help you master Photoshop. Let's say that you find an action that creates a texture that you really love, and you want to know how it was made. Just open the action to see the steps to make it. They appear in order of application from the first command at the top to the last command at the bottom.

Occasionally, some individual steps will also have a down arrow next to their names. For these steps, you can click the down arrow to open them and see the various settings in that step. For example, if there were a step that used the Gaussian Blur filter, you could click the down arrow to open that step and see the Radius value that was used. This is a great way to peer behind the proverbial curtain in Photoshop and figure out how certain tricks are done.

Like most of the features discussed in this chapter, actions do take some extra time to set up, but they are a wise investment of your time. Practice creating and using them as much as you can.

 You can turn off individual steps, preventing them from being used in the action, by deselecting the checkmark to the left of the name of the step.

 Although most Photoshop features can be contained in actions, some cannot. These include manual creative tasks such as painting or drawing, among others.

The Automate Commands

Automation in Photoshop can also be accessed by going to the File menu, and then going to the Automate submenu. While you can't directly access actions and the steps that create them from the File | Automate menu, you will find an entirely new stash of special commands (see Figure 16-5) that do some pretty miraculous things with minimal input from you.

FIGURE **16-5** The File I Automate commands

Crop and Straighten Photos

With the increasing popularity of digital photography, this feature loses a little popularity. The Crop And Straighten Photos command solves a major problem with scanned photos. Typically, photos are scanned by haphazardly tossing them onto the scanning surface of a flatbed scanner. This results in the scan being one large image, with the scanned photos being amalgamated (see Figure 16-6).

The Crop And Straighten Photos command will look at a single layer and try to find the original photos contained within it. It will then extract the photos, creating a separate document for each of them. It will also straighten them. So, with this layer selected, I'll choose File | Crop And Straighten Photos. Figure 16-7 shows how great this feature works.

FIGURE 16-6 Scanned images usually look like this

Photomerge

Photomerge is another automated command in Photoshop. Photomerge is intended for creating a single panoramic shot from multiple images. Panoramic images are very wide images that are typically of landscapes.

However, I like to use this feature for other purposes. If you want to create a large poster or billboard from a digital image, you'll probably have to stretch the image a great deal to make it large enough to fill large-format media. But if you take multiple close-up pictures of something, and then have Photoshop combine them into one large image, you might not have to scale it up, or at least scale it up quite so much.

Take, for example, the images seen in Figure 16-8. These were some photos I recently took in Washington, DC, while I was there teaching a class.

I usually try to pack as light as I can when I travel, so I took my camera's smallest lens. The lens size is 50 mm, which is ideal for shooting objects that are a few feet in front of you. To take good pictures of large buildings like this, you would need a lens with a wider viewing angle than the one I used. So, I took these pictures of different parts of the Lincoln Memorial, knowing that I could bring them into Photoshop and use the Photomerge command to automatically stitch them together.

You can use Photomerge by going to File | Automate | Photomerge. In the Photomerge dialog box, you can choose the images to merge together. They don't have to be currently open in Photoshop. To use other files on your computer, click the Browse button to locate them and use them in Photomerge. Or, click Add Open Files to use files already open in Photoshop. On the left side of the dialog box, you can select a method that Photoshop will use to merge the images. I find that Auto almost

FIGURE 16-7 After I run the Crop And Straighten Photos command, the photos are straightened and placed into separate documents.

always gets me the results I'm looking for. Once the files are loaded in this dialog box, click OK to have Photoshop merge these images. Be patient, as this process can take a while. Photoshop doesn't shrink any of your images, so the final composite is usually much larger than any individual image. Figure 16-9 shows the final Photomerge result. Notice how the Layers panel contains all four original images, with layer masks on them to blend them together. Spectacular.

Tip Many additional automation features that were once in Photoshop have now been moved to Adobe Bridge. You may consider investigating the help documentation for Adobe Bridge to find out what is available to you.

FIGURE 16-8 Multiple images of the Lincoln Memorial

FIGURE 16-9 The final Photomerge result

Saving Dialog Settings

This last method of automating is really not considered an automation feature per se. But it can save you so much time in the long run that it's very topical to this discussion. Most of the more advanced dialog boxes—especially those for color correcting, such as Hue/Saturation and Levels—allow you to save your settings and then reload them. I realize that, as with actions, this might take a little bit of extra setup time. But, as with actions, the reward is well worth it.

Let's see how to do this using Hue/Saturation as our example. Most effects and filters that allow you to save your settings have buttons that are clearly marked for saving and loading presets. When some effects are used in the Adjustments panel, you'll need to go to the Adjustments panel fly-out menu to access preset saving and loading options.

I have, in Figure 16-10, the original image I'll be using. This is another shot of the Lincoln Memorial, this time taken from the inside.

FIGURE 16-10 The original image

Apply a Hue/Saturation adjustment from the Adjustments panel. Make a significant change to your image. I'll select the Colorize check box, reduce the Saturation value, and change the Hue value to a greenish-blue color, as shown in Figure 16-11.

Next, I'll go to the Adjustments panel fly-out menu to choose to save these settings as a preset (see Figure 16-12). These settings are then saved as a file in the AHU format.

FIGURE 16-12 Save your Hue/Saturation settings by going to the fly-out menu of the Adjustments panel.

Expanded View

Save Hue/Saturation Preset...
Load Hue/Saturation Preset...
Delete Current Preset

Reset Hue/Saturation

Brightness/Contrast
Levels
Curves
Exposure

Vibrance
Hue/Saturation
Color Balance
Black & White
Photo Filter
Channel Mixer

Invert
Posterize
Threshold
Gradient Map
Selective Color

Close
Close Tab Group

FIGURE **16-13** Another image that is currently effect-free

Next, I'll open another image (see Figure 16-13) that I want to use these settings on.

To this new image, I'll apply a Hue/Saturation adjustment again. But instead of fiddling with the settings until I get it to look right, I'll just go back to my Adjustments panel fly-out menu and select Load Hue/Saturation Preset. Navigate to your saved AHU file, and click OK. Figure 16-14 shows the results. Now I have two images that will look like they belong together. I can combine them into the same layout, where they will match each other. Or, I can just relish the fact that it took me only a split second to apply all of these settings.

FIGURE 16-14 The new image, after applying the Hue/Saturation preset we created

17

Making a Living Using Photoshop

How to...

- Get a job that uses Photoshop
- Get the education you need for your career
- Use a portfolio
- Use certifications
- Use internships
- Acclimate to the culture of many digital art jobs

Now that you've seen what Photoshop can do, you may be wondering how you can play with Photoshop all day long and also get paid for it. You're not alone. Many people quickly feel the pull of Photoshop's addictive tentacles after they start playing around with it for more than a few minutes. So we're going to finish out this book in an unconventional way—by answering some of your Photoshop career questions.

You probably have a lot of questions in this area. What kind of education do you need to get started? You're a 55-year-old construction worker—is it too late for you to switch careers? What kind of art talent do you need? What type of photography experience do you need? Where can you get a job? What types of jobs are out there?

Obviously, we could spend weeks answering the preceding questions. I'll do my best to condense the highlights into this chapter. Remember that this is just helpful advice. I'm not the expert when it comes to every job out there. No one is. Photoshop has only been around since 1990 (publicly, anyway). So, as of this writing, the most seasoned of all professional Photoshop users has only 19 years of experience, and this entire industry is new and constantly evolving.

Can You Do This?

Before we really get into the nuts and bolts, I just want to make sure it's clear to you that you can do this. When I decided to drop out of my boring psychology major to pursue the exhilarating digital graphic arts field, no digital graphic arts field existed. Computers were just starting to be commonplace in colleges, and the digital graphic designer job path wasn't clearly defined.

What was worse for me is that I don't have any natural drawing talent. At all. I would go to some of my earlier teachers, and they would tell me that I could never make a living with Photoshop, that I just didn't have the talent for it. But I persisted. I desperately wanted to be a digital artist. I've always loved art and artistic things. I was terrible with a computer, but since my dad is a wizard of nerdy computer things, I figured I could channel at least some remnant of his genius genes. So, I wouldn't give up, and I wouldn't take no for an answer. When I would hit a career wall, I would climb it, go around it, or dig under it. If you have that attitude, you will be successful. I've now created advertising for major Hollywood movies and created art for Paramount, Warner Brothers, Disney, Lockheed Martin, United Way, and more. It's a great feeling to go into a retail store's DVD section and see art that you helped to create. The teachers that said I couldn't do it were wrong. Don't get discouraged. There are solutions to every problem you will encounter.

What Kind of Education Do You Need?

This is a valid concern. For most careers, the amount of schooling required to obtain a job in that field is critically important. With Photoshop, however, the field is so new that there isn't much in the way of education out there. As far as I'm aware, there are no college degrees in Photoshop.

Most employers are far more concerned with your artistic talent than with your education. If you have a PhD in the art world, but can't make a decent selection in Photoshop, or can't organize information for a magazine ad, then your degree doesn't mean anything. On the other hand, if you're really talented, you might get a job without ever taking a class. I know a young man who is extraordinarily talented in the digital arts.

He started selling hand-drawn portraits when he was still in high school. By the time he graduated high school, he had one of the most prestigious companies in the video game industry paying him to move from California to New York to work for them. Not only did this kid not have any schooling under his belt (other than high school), but he also didn't have any job experience whatsoever.

For the jobs that do require a college degree, employers are almost always looking for a degree in fine arts. If you're a talented artist, it doesn't take much more than a book (like this one) to bring you up to speed with a software program. But if you're a master of Photoshop and don't know basic rules of composition or how to use colors together effectively, then your Photoshop knowledge is irrelevant.

Your Portfolio

My friend got his dream job because of his portfolio. A portfolio is a collection of your best work. It is the thing that defines you. For most employers, this is by far your most important qualification.

 For those of you seeking to work in the world of video, motion graphics, or 3D, you will create a video portfolio, called a *demo reel.*

When preparing their portfolios, many artists include every single job they've ever done. This is not a good idea. As Apple demonstrated with their revolutionary iPod commercials, less is more. Have a handful of your best pieces, but don't let your future employer know that you make mediocre art. Everything should be as impressive as it can possibly be.

Also, if you're going for a particular type of job (advertising, for example), then try to show your best work for that job. Your Jackson Pollock art won't help you land the job doing architectural visualization work.

Certifications

While they can never come close to being a substitute for a good portfolio, industry certifications can sometimes convince employers that you at least know what you're talking about. Adobe offers several levels of certification ranging from Adobe Certified Associate (for entry level Photoshop work), Adobe

Certified Expert (a much harder test), and Adobe Certified Instructor (an Adobe Certified Expert with certified teaching skills). For more information on these tests, check out Adobe.com. I've also created a free video podcast on the subject, which can be found at www.chadandtoddcast.com.

Internships

Some employers want more than anything else to see that you have experience working in their field before they will hire you. I've seen so many kids go to college, pay tens of thousands of dollars for a quality education, and have a killer portfolio, only to be refused work at every turn because they lack experience. Lacking experience is one of life's painful ironies. Jobs require experience, but you can't get experience because you can't get a job because you can't get experience because you can't get a job, and so on.

One way to solve that problem is by taking an internship. Many business owners love the opportunity to exploit the talents of the less experienced. Hence, society has created internships. Basically, you're a glorified volunteer. Although some internships do pay a little cash, most do not. You are essentially trading in your wages for job experience. This is a tough sacrifice to make, but for many struggling digital artists, the sacrifice is worth it.

What Types of Jobs Are Available?

This truly is an impossible question to answer. So many jobs out there use Photoshop. Ready for the longest sentence of the book? Here goes. Photoshop is used in fashion design, photography and photographic retouching, architectural design and previsualization (to show what buildings will look like before they're built), magazines, ads, newspapers, web design, designing software interfaces (what the buttons and other elements look like), motion graphics and animation, visual effects for Hollywood movies, packaging, lenticular printing, images for cell phones and other mobile devices, logo creation, photo archival, medical imaging, engineering, textile and fabric design, and creating textures for 3D objects for films, video games, court scene reenactments, scientific renderings, and more.

The Culture of Digital Art Jobs

I don't mean to generalize here. Every employer is different. But in most cases, jobs in the digital arts realm are a little more laid back and casual. Usually, a *lot* more casual. Some art studios will have game rooms, TV rooms, video game rooms, and other entertainment that employees can use whenever they want to unwind. Pixar has paper airplane contests. One company (Big Spaceship) even allows pets and encourages goofing off on company time. Art studios usually don't have dress codes of any kind. It's not uncommon to walk into an art studio and see a couple of kids with blue Mohawks, or to have a meeting with executives with everyone in sandals. Coworkers are usually friendly and open.

The obvious benefit of this is that work is a great experience. Or, it's at least better than most other jobs. Who wouldn't want to go to work somewhere like Big Spaceship, where the environment is so relaxed and conducive to creativity? Wise employers understand that stressed artists usually don't produce very much inspired content.

The downside of this environment is that it may not be what you're used to. If you're a jerk, you'll have a difficult time working in an environment like this. If you have a tough time suppressing your anger issues, no one will want to play foosball with you. And that's a good way to find yourself out of work.

Some people (like me) love to be able to do whatever the heck they want. Most artists really flourish in such an environment. But some people need more structure. I should also point out that not all graphics design jobs are this laid back. If you work in an industry that puts more focus on deadlines than art (like a newspaper), there probably won't be a pinball machine in the break room. This is a small issue for some and a major issue for others.

Where Do I Find Work?

For most (but absolutely not all) users of Photoshop, it is probably most common to find work with those who do print work. Print shops and ad agencies are a great place to begin looking. They can at least give you a better idea of the qualifications and salary of jobs that use Photoshop in the area. Remember to be respectful. I get dozens (sometimes hundreds) of e-mails every day from people who want me to give them free one-on-one training, or to fix their technical issues, or to help them get a job. In their zeal, they sometimes forget that while I would love nothing more than to help the world all day every day, I also have bills to pay and a family to feed. If someone on the other line is kind enough to donate work time to answer your questions, be brief, organized, and grateful.

For all Photoshop users, here is my advice. Think of your dream job. You don't have to do this today or by the end of the week. Take some time. Seriously. If you could rub a magic lamp and obtain any job using Photoshop, what would you be doing? Once you've thought of your dream job, do some research and find out who does what you want to do. As we'll discuss in a moment, the Internet is the greatest resource you could ever hope for. Then, once you've found the company that offers the dream job you're looking for, call their HR department and ask what it takes to get your job. Or, better yet, try to find this information on the company's web site.

The Best Resources of All Time

Succeeding in this industry takes some great art skills. But getting started in this industry takes some great detective skills. You have to be willing to do your homework. If you know someone who has succeeded and is willing to help you, then great. Ask them for advice and help. But you still need to have the willpower and determination to try and find these answers for yourself. Often when people e-mail me looking for quick answers on getting started in this business, I'll give them the links to great web training, tutorials, or other information. Sometimes they will be grateful that they have a place to start. But many (most?) will complain because I didn't take the time to do all the work for them in my e-mail. I worry about the future success of people who aren't willing to put effort into their own careers. Especially because digital art jobs are fun. A lot of potential employees are out there who are willing to do their homework if it means landing their dream job.

There are a couple of great resources to help you get started. One we've already talked about is Google.com. Google has the answer to almost every problem and question you've ever had. Self-starters and those committed to this field of work are never stuck as long as they have Google.com.

The second resource is another web resource: Wikipedia.org. You might not know all you want to know about color, or the EPS file format, even after reading this amazing book. Wikipedia has answers to little weird techy things like that. It's a great resource for digital artists. It can also help you know common slang and lingo used in the industry you're trying to get into. For example, many 3D applications contain basic 3D objects (cone, sphere, and so on), but they also usually include a teapot. Any idea why? Teapots have a special place in the history of 3D graphics. Actually, one special teapot, the Utah teapot, is at the heart of it. I'll leave that to you to look up, but I will tell you that the answer is on Wikipedia. If that teapot were to come up in a conversation with someone who worked in the world of 3D, it might be a good tidbit of information to know.

Conventions and User Groups

As in any artistic field, networking is a key ingredient to success. As they say in show business, it's all who you know. This is extremely true. I've worked at companies that turned down really talented, qualified people for jobs. And then, when I said that I had a friend/family member that didn't know anything but needed a job, they were hired on the spot. It may sound unconventional, but being a nice, affable person can get you really far, especially in this field.

A great place to practice your people skills is to go to conventions and user groups. Conventions are held frequently in many major cities. Some, like Macworld, are only held in one place. But if the convention is big enough in the industry (like Macworld is), then it can be worth the time and money to travel there to learn from the seminars and meet experts and other users. User groups are literally groups of users. There probably is a Photoshop user group somewhere near you. And if there isn't one, start one! User groups are communities of users who get together to talk about their industries and pertinent issues. People in user groups can share ideas and business contacts, start businesses together, help each other find work, discuss industry trends, and alert each other to upcoming industry events.

Who's the Boss?

In this chapter, we've mostly looked at how to find a job. But the fact of the matter is, many artists are their own boss. Being self-employed is obviously a scary endeavor. There are usually no benefits such as health care or retirement, the paychecks are unsteady, and you don't get vacation days or sick days. To be self-employed, you must be a self-starter.

But I can tell you from personal experience that being self-employed has its advantages. That's how I've chosen to live my life. I love the freedom that I have, not having to go to work. I spend most of my days playing with my wife and my kids. I can take on extra jobs because I can work as much as I need to. I can also spend more time pursuing hobbies or learning other skills. I can also give myself raises whenever I want (clients willing, of course). I am a self-starter, so this lifestyle works well for me. But that may not be the case for everyone.

If you are new to this industry, you may want to get a job just so you can get some real-world experience. I was an employee for two years for another company, and I loved my time there. I learned a great deal from the other artists and marketing people who worked there.

If you are curious about firing your boss and going self-employed, you don't have to quit your job tomorrow. You can start working nights and weekends on your own, building up a client base. Or perhaps, you can spend the time learning new skills. If you don't quite have enough energy to work a full day at the office, and then come home and work more at night, then being self-employed probably isn't your thing for right now. When your side income starts getting to a point where it can support you, then you can better evaluate whether working for yourself is really the best option for you.

Index

WITHDRAWN